The CaReeR CowaRd's Guide™ to
Interviewing

Sensible Strategies for Overcoming Job Search Fears

jist Works
America's Career Publisher™

Katy Piotrowski, M.Ed.

D1110778

The Career Coward's Guide to Interviewing

© 2007 by Katy Piotrowski

Published by JIST Works, an imprint of JIST Publishing, Inc.
8902 Otis Avenue
Indianapolis, IN 46216-1033
Phone: 1-800-648-JIST   Fax: 1-800-JIST-FAX   E-mail: info@jist.com

Visit our Web site at www.jist.com for information on JIST, free job search tips, book chapters, and ordering instructions for our many products! For free information on 14,000 job titles, visit www.careeroink.com.

See the back of this book for additional titles in the *Career Coward's* series. Quantity discounts are available for JIST books. Have future editions of JIST books automatically delivered to you on publication through our convenient standing order program. Please call our Sales Department at 1-800-648-5478 for a free catalog and more information.

Trade Product Manager: Lori Cates Hand
Cover Designer: Trudy Coler
Cover Illustration: © Masterfile
Interior Designer: Amy Peppler Adams
Page Layout: Toi Davis
Proofreader: Jeanne Clark
Indexer: Cheryl Lenser

Printed in the United States of America
12 11 10 09 08 07   9 8 7 6 5 4 3 2 1

   Library of Congress Cataloging-in-Publication Data
Piotrowski, Katy, 1962-
   The career coward's guide to interviewing : sensible strategies for overcoming job search fears / by Katy Piotrowski.
      p. cm.
   Includes index.
   ISBN 978-1-59357-389-8 (alk. paper)
   1. Employment interviewing. I. Title.
   HF5549.5.I6P563 2007
   650.14'4--dc22

                                              2006037966

ISBN 978-1-59357-389-8

About This Book

Does the thought of interviewing for a job terrify you? Do you have great skills and experience to offer, yet lose your confidence when it comes to communicating those strengths to an employer? Do you wish you had a proven, simple process that would significantly increase your success in interviews?

If you answered, "Yes!" to these questions, this book is for you. *The Career Coward's Guide to Interviewing* was written for the talented, deserving job searcher who has so much to share, yet struggles to promote him-or herself successfully in interviews. This book takes each stage of the interview process—from easy tips to increase the number of interviews you land; to how to prepare effectively for the interview; to how to deliver a dynamite, self-assured performance throughout the interview—and breaks it into easy, doable steps that allow you to quickly build your interviewing skills and confidence.

Not sure how to execute a winning handshake? Wish you knew how to keep your self-belief high, even when you start to panic? Want to learn how to negotiate competitive pay, even though you might be shaking inside? All the answers, and myriad other outstanding tips and techniques, are included in this book.

If you've looked at other interviewing guides and quickly felt intimidated or confused, then this book's clear, simple-to-use style will be just right for you. *The Career Coward's Guide to Interviewing* lets you jump in just where you need help and then walks you through a friendly, effective, step-by-step process for learning what you need to know. Does it work? You bet! As a career counselor who has helped thousands of career cowards since 1992, I've seen first-hand which interviewing strategies work best when the tension is high—and I've summarized those techniques in this book, just for you.

So quit cowering in the corner, afraid to put your best self out there for employers to see. Begin right now to improve your interviewing skills, and then look forward to achieving the career results you deserve.

—Katy P.

Dedication

*To Melanie and Nat, who saw past
the coward in me and helped me find
the courage in myself!*

Contents

Acknowledgments

I'd like to thank the following people who helped me arrive at the point of being able to write this book: my parents, Doris McGinley and Peter Patrick, who always told me that I could do anything I wanted to try; my long-time counselor, Melanie Nickerson, who helped me believe that I actually could make my dreams happen; my husband, Pete Piotrowski, who has stood next to me, picked me up, and nudged me forward (depending on what I needed) and made sure I had the right tools to get the job done; my daughter Ada and son JP, who continually give me opportunities to learn and grow and love me even when I make mistakes; Nat Kees, my graduate professor at Colorado State University, who saw and believed in my vision before I even had it in focus; Richard Bolles, Rich Feller, Dick Knowdell, and Daniel Porot, four career-industry gurus who have given me the essential career tools I rely on every day; Lori Frieling, Jim Caron, Bob Baun, and Dave Grieling, who gave me my first opportunities to write professionally; Louise Kursmark, an author who inspired me; Dana Klausmeyer, Ruth Pancratz, and Brad Shannon, colleagues who supported me; Cynthia Morris, the writing coach who guided me; Lori Cates Hand, the editor at JIST who said, "Yes!" to my proposal; my friends Karen Thompson, Lisa Sullender, and Marybeth Van Fossen, who are my tireless cheerleaders; and last, but never least, my (sometimes cowardly) clients, who allow me to ply my passion toward helping them make their career dreams come true.

Conquering the Career Coward in You

Are *you* a Career Coward when it comes to interviews?

Does the thought of sitting in front of a hiring manager talking about yourself, trying to make yourself sound good, cause your heart to pound? Do seemingly simple tasks such as introducing yourself, shaking hands, and making small talk cause you to sweat?

When it comes to the question, "Tell me about yourself," do you panic, wondering what in the world you should say? Do you typically leave an interview frustrated with yourself because you *could* have said so much more to promote yourself, but instead, your brain seemed to have forgotten how to function when you needed it most?

Do you hold back on job searching more actively because interviews are a stressor you'd just rather not deal with at all?

If you answered "yes" to most of these questions, then you *are* a Career Coward.

A Career Coward is someone who knows he or she is capable of greater career successes, but feels terrified and paralyzed to take steps to move forward because he or she is afraid to fail or look like a fool.

Yet if you're reading this book, most likely you're ready to tackle your fears of interviewing and finally move ahead in your career. This book, written just for Career Cowards who struggle with interviewing, is a great way to get there. Each chapter provides you with techniques that have been tried, tested, and perfected on thousands of other Career Cowards. And to make learning this valuable information enjoyable and successful, each chapter includes these fun and easy-to-read sections:

- A **"Risk It or Run From It"** status box, which provides you vital information at the start of each chapter. Each status box includes this data:

  - *Risk Rating:* From "No risk at all" to "This is a deal breaker!" you'll quickly see how harmless or hazardous each step will be.

  - *Payoff Potential:* Find out what's in it for you if you *do* decide to take the risk and complete the step. The payoff may be enough to push you through any fear that's holding you back.

  - *Time to Complete:* Whether it's a few minutes or a few hours, you'll know in advance how much time each activity will take.

  - *Bailout Strategy:* Absolutely refuse to put in the time or take the risk for a particular step? You have other options; find out what they are.

  - *The "20 Percent Extra" Edge:* Learn how braving the recommended steps will give you a significant advantage over your competition.

  - *"Go For It!" Bonus Activity:* Feeling really courageous? Take your success even further with this suggested activity.

- A **"How To"** section, which provides clear, motivating instructions for each activity.

- **Panic Points** note boxes, which pop up at the places in the process where people freak out, offering quick encouragement to get past the panic.

- Information about **"Why It's Worth Doing,"** which helps you to understand the purpose behind each interviewing recommendation.

- An encouraging **"Career Champ Profile,"** which describes a real-life example of a Career Coward who succeeded after conquering a challenging interviewing fear.

- The **"Core Courage Concept,"** which boils down the chapter's key points into an inspiring message.

- And a **"Confidence Checklist,"** which provides you an at-a-glance review of the section's primary action items.

Feeling encouraged? Great! Now find out how the techniques described in this book helped a Career Coward just like you.

The Story of Kirsten, a Career Coward

Interviewing was a terrifying experience for Kirsten. She'd recently finished a master's degree in technical journalism and knew she was now qualified for better, higher-paying positions than the community college English teaching jobs she'd held for the last 10 years. Her resume was working; she'd applied for six tech writing openings in the last two months and had received three calls for interviews. But all of the interviews had been disasters.

As each interviewer asked her questions, Kirsten's heart would pound and her brain would freeze. She stumbled through her responses, barely making eye contact with the interviewer. She knew she was doing an awful job of presenting her strengths and experience, and she couldn't wait for the interviews to end.

With each interviewing failure, Kirsten's confidence dipped a little lower. It had gotten to the point that she was now hesitant to submit her resume for *any* openings, knowing that applying for a job might lead to another interview.

When Kirsten and I met to begin working on her interviewing skills, she told me about her frustrations: "I *know* I can do a great job for a company, but I'm terrible at communicating that to them. I've got great qualifications, but I don't know how to express what I can do. I'm sure that my writing skills from my other jobs are transferable to technical writing positions, but what do I say to prove that to them?

"Another problem is that I know I'm *supposed* to prepare for an interview…but I don't know how. I've tried anticipating their questions, but so far I've been a miserable failure at that guessing game. The whole experience makes me so nervous. I even had my doctor write me a prescription for something that would calm me down. Well, the pills did make me less nervous, but I *still* didn't know what to say."

I suggested a plan to help Kirsten overcome her fears and begin presenting herself more successfully in interviews. She first needed to prove to herself—through concrete evidence—that she was qualified for the jobs she wanted. To do this, I had her pick a position that she'd interviewed poorly for in the last few months and analyze the top skills and experience needed for the position. She chose the ElektraTech technical writing job and wrote out three top qualifications:

1. Someone who could write about their technology in a clear, understandable way.

2. Someone who could work well in a team environment.

3. Someone who had a proven track record for completing projects on time.

"Are you good at these things?" I asked Kirsten. "Yes!" she said emphatically. "I'm *great* at those things. I just don't know how to make the interviewer believe that, too."

I then asked Kirsten to come up with three examples of times when she'd written about technology in a clear, understandable way. "Oh, easy. One time was with my master's thesis. Another time was when I got a contract job to write a technical manual for a software company. And a third was in my last teaching job, when the department head had me document the process the administrative team used to enter information into the new school database." I then asked Kirsten to choose one of those examples and tell me, in detail, about what had happened.

She described how one of the schools where she taught English had purchased new database software, and even though the software manufacturer had trained the administrators on how to use it, the team was making lots of data-entry mistakes. They were being inconsistent in how they entered information, and it was causing problems with student records.

The department head asked Kirsten to study the data-entry process, and to document the correct steps in a manual so that the admin team could learn and follow the proper procedures. For a period of five days, Kirsten watched the team enter data and asked lots of questions to understand the possible situations that might arise when entering information into the database. She also verified correct data-entry procedures with the administrative supervisor, taking lots of detailed, accurate notes with each conversation.

Over the next week, Kirsten wrote up an outline of what she perceived to be the correct steps, ran them by the supervisor, and tested the processes with a few of the administrators. When she was confident that she had an accurate process defined, she documented all of the information in a 30-page instruction manual. She then had two administrators use the manual for 10 days, making notes about things that confused them and pointing out errors. Kirsten then incorporated these changes into an updated version and put together some PowerPoint slides for the administrative supervisor to use when he trained his team on how to use the manual.

The manual was then introduced to the team. Within a week, data-entry errors dropped to almost zero. Kirsten also heard from several admin team members that they were relieved to have a clear, understandable manual to follow because it made their jobs a lot easier. Kirsten even received a letter from the dean of the school, thanking her for her excellent work.

As she told me this story, Kirsten's eyes sparkled and she smiled widely. She was enthusiastic and convincing. "Wow," I said. "That's an *excellent* example. I'd hire you!"

"Yeah," Kirsten said, her eyes looking sad again and an edge of frustration creeping back into her voice, "but I *never* get to tell a story like that in an interview. Either they don't ask me a question like you did, or I freeze up and can't remember the details!"

"Well, we're going to work together so that in interviews, you'll have *plenty* of opportunities to tell great stories just like that one. You'll soon feel as excited and comfortable talking with a hiring manager as you do with me." I then assigned Kirsten homework: To create a database of success stories like the one she'd just told me, following a specific format that included information about

1. What the problem or challenge was that she was faced with

2. How she solved it

3. Proof that her result was successful

She brought her database of examples to our next meeting. "This was fun," she told me, laying her written examples on my desk. "Already I feel more confident, having all of this evidence written down." We then spent the next few meetings practicing answers to questions she might be asked in an interview, using the success story examples she'd prepared. With each practice session, Kirsten's confidence grew.

A few weeks later, Kirsten received a call for an interview with one of the top technical companies in the area. "I'm a little nervous, but I'm also looking forward to trying some of the new interviewing techniques we've been practicing," Kirsten explained. "You're definitely prepared," I told her. "Just remember: Anytime you start to panic, recall all of your accomplishments. They're evidence that you're great at what you do."

The morning after the interview, Kirsten called me with an update: "You won't believe this!" she began, with excitement in her voice, "I interviewed for that tech writing job. I was nervous at the start, but after a minute or two, I started having *fun!* I was able to respond successfully to each question, and I felt as though they were seeing the real Kirsten, not some nervous, doped up version.

"At the end of the interview, they told me they'd let me know by next Monday. But by the time I'd arrived back home, they'd already called and left a message on my answering machine, making me an offer—for *twice* as much as I've been making as a teacher!"

Kirsten, a former Career Coward, went from having very little belief in her interviewing skills, to building her confidence in her ability to promote herself, to landing a great job. Now you'll learn how to do the same!

Part 1

Land and Prep for a Fantastic (and Fearless) Interview

Chapter 1

Set Yourself Up to Succeed

I t's probably no surprise to you that when it comes to interviewing, you're your biggest asset *and* worst enemy. When you believe in yourself, you—more than anyone else—are capable of promoting yourself effectively. Yet when you're scared or nervous, your confidence can crash, making it nearly impossible to represent yourself in a positive way.

Your challenge (and this book will help you accomplish it) is to learn how to minimize the times when you feel unsure of yourself and maximize the times when you feel confident—so that you can achieve the best possible interview results.

To get started on this path toward interviewing success, you'll first define the job you really want and then picture yourself interviewing successfully for it.

Risk It or Run From It?

- **Risk Rating:** Very low. You're just dreaming and visualizing at this point—something you can do in private.

- **Payoff Potential:** Huge! From great plans come great results.

(continued)

(continued)

- **Time to Complete:** 15–60 minutes.

- **Bailout Strategy:** Planning and visualizing aren't essential. You can skip this step and wing it…but you'll have better results if you think about what you want to achieve before you begin your search. With the low risk and high payoff potential of this step, why not go for it? (Do it over a coffee. It'll seem like a treat.)

- **The "20 Percent Extra" Edge:** Having a vision for the kind of job you want, and believing that you can perform well in an interview, will set you apart from the crowd.

- **"Go For It!" Bonus Activity:** Read through the interviewing visualization exercise at least once a day for a month to program your brain for success.

How to Create Your Interviewing Success

Improving your skills in interviewing will take motivation and commitment. Are you ready to begin? If you could use a little extra inspiration, the following activities will help you get pumped and prepared for interviewing success.

Be Inspired to Risk and Achieve

Remember the last time you really, really wanted something, and you found yourself jumping through higher and higher hoops to get it? Years ago, when I discovered the field of career counseling and decided to change careers to begin a new profession, I found myself taking risks I never imagined I would. Typically a play-it-safe kinda girl determined to protect my secure little world, I started doing things like quitting my great-paying marketing job and applying to graduate school in a state thousands of miles away, with no job, friends, or family (and only a huge tuition bill!) in sight. I also found myself taking risks I'd never done before to set up job interviews. I needed to create some income so that I could continue to go to school, so I energetically contacted professor after professor in an attempt to line up a teaching assistantship. I was more persistent than I'd ever been in my life, but I hadn't gone crazy; rather, I was *inspired!*

Inspiration can be the catalyst that pushes you to try new things. Find something you're motivated to obtain, and you may also find yourself accomplishing feats you never believed were possible. So, what *is* your career inspiration? What career hope do you have that will help motivate you to take the risks necessary to become great at interviewing? Define this for yourself, and you'll already be halfway to the goal.

Define the Job You Want, Then Land Interviews!

Begin to create a picture for yourself of the job you'd really love to have. Ask yourself, "What would I do for work if I could choose any specialty? What would I change or add to my current job if I could? What talents do I possess that I'd like to use more in my work? Who do I know with a job that I'd love, and what are they doing?" Aim to create a list of three to ten specific aspects of a career you'd love to have, such as writing, working with numbers, or designing things.

Panic Point! When your self-doubt starts to creep in, taunting you with, "What's the point of creating a career wish list? I'll never land a great job...it's safer to stay where I am," remind yourself that at this stage in the process, you're just dreaming. You won't be making any life-changing decisions right now; you're just taking baby steps. If things start to seem too scary or overwhelming, you can put on the brakes. So permit yourself to take the first step to create a list of your career hopes; then prioritize the factors that are most important to you.

Brainstorm potential jobs that involve the skills and responsibilities you have identified. If you're not yet sure which types of jobs would allow you to apply the skills you'd like to use, review potential job descriptions through an online job site such as www.monster.com.

Simply type in keywords from your career wish list, such as "Writing, travel, organizing" and click "Search" to view jobs that include those tasks. At this point, don't worry about selecting any geographic preferences—your primary goal is to get ideas about potential job titles and sample job descriptions, not to actually apply for specific openings. As you locate appealing job descriptions, make a list of the job titles that seem to be a good fit for you.

Now that you're beginning to get a picture of jobs and careers that would truly inspire you, take steps that will move you closer to landing interviews for those positions.

1. **Create a resume that emphasizes your skills related to your target position.** Include evidence of your relevant experience, and organize your resume to paint a picture of where you're going rather than where you've been. (A functional resume format, which emphasizes your relevant skills rather than a chronological list of your job titles and responsibilities, is often a better choice if you're making a career change.) If you're not sure how to create an effective resume that highlights your background related to a specific career target, hire a professional resume writer. This person will be skilled at asking you the right questions to draw out the experience you possess related to your career goals.

2. **Research a list of potential employers.** Ask yourself, "In which types of companies would this job exist?" Use the yellow pages, business directories (available at library reference desks), and the Internet to create a list of 20 to 50 potential employers. Create a record of each organization's contact information, products and services offered, and key hiring managers.

> **Tip:** Keep in mind that 75 percent of us work at companies with fewer than 25 employees. So as you review lists of organizations, be sure to consider smaller employers as well as larger, more well-known businesses.

3. **Use effective job search techniques to land interviews.** Ninety percent of job searchers rely on the help-wanted ads to find job openings, yet nearly 70 percent of positions are never advertised! Smarter job searchers send their resumes directly to potential employers even if no positions are advertised, and network with friends and colleagues to learn about job leads before the jobs are posted to the public.

4. **Stick with your job search long enough to land some great interviews.** Keep in mind that, on average, it takes about 10 attempts (submitting your resume to 10 organizations, or networking with 10 colleagues) to land one job interview. Give yourself time to succeed before saying, "It didn't work!"

Why It's Worth Doing

Visualizing your ideal job helps you see yourself differently. Typically, we can't change the result until we begin seeing and doing things in a different way. Dreaming and visualizing are the first steps!

Career Champ Profile: Monica

Monica was employed in a social-services position that had become boring to her. "It scares me to think about finding a job that I'd actually love. What if I write out what I want, work toward it, interview for it, and then don't get it? Then I wouldn't even have my dream anymore!" It seemed safer to Monica to not even risk dreaming about a better opportunity.

"How about if you let your dreams peek out of the shadows just a little," I encouraged her. "Later, if you decide that you want to tuck them safe inside again, that's okay." Monica agreed to daydream.

"If you could change one thing about your career, what would you change?" I asked her. Monica had an answer immediately. "I'd write more," she said. "What else?" I prompted. Monica continued listing her hopes, and within a few minutes we'd added more items to her wish list: Travel. Learning a second language. Becoming an expert on food. Soon a picture of attractive jobs started to appear.

Taking it to the next step, I asked Monica to tell me about experience she had that would qualify her for those kinds of jobs. At first Monica wasn't sure she had any relevant experience to share. "You're a member of a writing group, aren't you?" I asked. "Well, yes…" she answered. "Does that count?"

Soon Monica was able to recall several experiences in her background that were relevant to jobs that appealed to her. We used this information to build a database of examples that Monica could talk about in job interviews. And as the evidence of her experience grew, so did Monica's confidence. "Maybe I really *can* land a job I love!" she admitted excitedly. Monica was on her way.

Core Courage Concept

It can be scary to imagine and write down what you really want. But keep in mind that no one else needs to ever know your vision, unless you choose to share it. Yet if you give yourself permission to dream about the kind of job you'd really love to have, and picture yourself interviewing successfully for it, you increase your chances of actually moving on to the next step… and then the next step… so that eventually that great job *can* come into your life.

Confidence Checklist

☐ Be inspired to risk and achieve.

☐ Define the job you want, and then land interviews!

☐ Visualize yourself as an interviewing success.

Chapter 2

Understand the Hiring Manager's Perspective

When it comes to interviews, there are two sides to the story: the candidate's and the decision maker's. Although technically you can control only what happens on your side of the equation, it helps to understand the challenges the hiring manager may be facing as well. This allows you to help make the process easier for the decision maker, so that ultimately, he or she will want to hire you!

Risk It or Run From It?

- **Risk Rating:** There's no risk at all with this chapter—just important, enlightening information for you to enjoy.

- **Payoff Potential:** Massive. Understanding more about how a decision maker thinks, and how interview opportunities evolve, gives you a tremendous edge over other job seekers.

- **Time to Complete:** Only as long as it takes you to read this chapter.

- **Bailout Strategy:** You'll keep breathing without this information; but since the risk is nil and the payoff is great, why not read on?

(continued)

(continued)

- **The "20 Percent Extra" Edge:** Looking at the interviewing process from the decision maker's perspective helps you spot and respond more effectively to opportunities.

- **"Go For It!" Bonus Activity:** Think about three organizations where you'd like to have a job interview, even if there are no advertised openings, and attempt to set up a meeting with a decision maker at those organizations.

How to Read the Hiring Manager's Mind

Learn more about the hiring difficulties decision makers face—as well as ways that you can help make the process easier for them—and you'll achieve more successful interviewing results.

The following story illustrates a number of typical challenges a hiring manager may encounter.

Doug runs a marketing agency. Currently, five people work for him: an office manager, a creative director, a copywriter, and two account executives. But Doug's been losing sleep lately worrying about Brad, the copywriter on his team.

Brad has been with the agency for eight months. Doug hired him when Alisha, the former copywriter, moved to Greenland to pursue her life's dream of traveling and writing. Although Brad tries hard, he's just not working out. His copy lacks the "ummph" that would make the agency great. Brad's getting the job done...but just barely.

Doug would let Brad go if he had a better replacement, but right now Doug's thoughts are occupied with other things...like the best way to upgrade the business's accounting system, and how he can help the agency hang onto one of its most important accounts.

But one afternoon Doug finds a 9 x 12 envelope on his desk. Inside is a cover letter and resume from Tessa, a copywriter. Doug hadn't advertised for a new copywriter, but Tessa sent a resume anyway. And based on Tessa's writing, Doug has an idea that she's pretty talented. "Maybe I'll phone her tomorrow, to find out more," Doug decides. He sets the envelope aside, planning to get back to it soon.

Four days go by, however, with Doug doing his best to wade through accounting system decisions and find ways to keep his primo customer happy. Tessa's resume is by now long forgotten, buried under a pile of other "I'll get to it eventually" papers.

Checking his e-mail that day, Doug sees a message titled, "To Doug Barkley from Tessa Strelling." Reading the message, Doug discovers it's from the same Tessa who sent him the resume a few days before, following up on her mailing.

"I just wanted to make sure you received my information successfully. I'd like the chance to meet with you to introduce myself and see if there are ways that we can support each other in the future. If I don't hear from you in the next day or so, I'll phone you to make sure this e-mail got through."

Doug's opinion of Tessa is climbing even higher. "She seems to have her act together, checking back with me like this. Comes across as pretty confident, too." Doug hits the Reply button and sends her this message: "Tessa, I'd like to meet you, too. Any chance you could stop by this Friday sometime between 2 and 4 p.m.?" They agree on 2:30, and Doug goes back to fighting the fires roaring at his agency.

When she shows up on Friday promptly at 2:30, wearing a stylish navy suit and carrying a black leather portfolio, Doug is secretly thrilled that her appearance matches how he imagined she'd be: professional and friendly. But then Doug starts to panic. Tessa seems prepared, but he's not! After setting the appointment, Doug didn't give their interview a second thought. He doesn't even have a list of questions to ask her.

Going for the safe opener, Doug says, "Tell me about yourself." Tessa talks about where she was raised, her education, and her last two copywriting jobs. She tells Doug a very impressive story about a large campaign proposal she worked on last month, as the lead copywriter. That proposal landed her current employer a $3 million account.

Doug finds that talking with Tessa is easy. Even though he didn't have a prepared agenda, Tessa seems comfortable steering the conversation. She readily shares specific examples about her experience that relate to the projects that Doug's agency handles, making it easy for Doug to ask additional questions. She also mentions campaigns she knows Doug's agency created, commenting on the aspects of the marketing strategy that she liked best.

Nearing the end of their conversation, Tessa asks Doug to keep her in mind if there's ever a need in their agency for a copywriter. Not ready to make a commitment (there's still the Brad issue to sort out…) Doug replies, "You bet!" "Here's my contact information," Tessa says, handing over a simple card with her phone and e-mail information.

Doug sits in his office for a few minutes after his conversation with Tessa, thinking about how much he would love to have Tessa on his team. Then Paula, his creative director, interrupts his daydream. "Doug, about the Bluebird Systems campaign…."

Three days later, lost in the demands of the day, Doug's conversation with Tessa seems a distant memory. When Tessa does cross his mind, Doug thinks, "Maybe Brad's not that bad after all. The last ad copy he wrote for Bluebird showed promise. And changing a team member would mean a lot of extra hassle for me."

"Mail call!" Stella, the office manager sings out shortly after lunch, dropping a stack on Doug's desk. "Hmmm, a hand-addressed note. That looks more interesting than the bills…" Doug thinks, choosing that one to open first.

In neat, steady handwriting, Tessa had written, "Dear Doug, Thanks so much for your time last Friday. I enjoyed learning more about your agency. It's obvious that there's a great future ahead for your company. I'd love to be a part of making that future a reality. If your needs ever change, please keep me in mind. Sincerely, Tessa"

Maybe the hassle of switching copywriters would be worth it. Maybe tomorrow Doug would do some serious thinking about letting Brad go.

But it would be two weeks before Doug would do that serious thinking. Brad had just turned in copy for an important proposal, and Doug was disappointed. "This isn't acceptable," thinks Doug. Frustrated, Doug hunts through his business cards looking for Tessa's. Finding it in his stack, he dials her number and leaves a message, "Tessa, I'd like to set a time to talk about creating a position for you here…."

As you can see, Tessa's timing for meeting Doug turned out to be ideal. Tessa wanted a new job, and by chance, Doug needed her, too. Tessa was able to orchestrate an interview and land a job offer, even though a job ad was never posted!

Situations that result in hiring opportunities are constantly evolving. The "traditional" interview process that we imagine—where a company manager decides he or she needs to hire a person; writes up a detailed job description; posts it in newspapers and online to solicit applicants; and interviews them in a thorough, orderly process—is a rarity.

More often, circumstances like the one between Doug and Tessa motivate a hiring change. Opportunities pop up quickly. And if you've mastered some simple yet powerful interviewing skills, you'll be better able to promote yourself successfully, no matter how nervous you feel inside.

Why It's Worth Doing

Decision makers—those people who are in charge of saying "yea" or "nay" about hiring a candidate—are constantly faced with hiring choices. "Should I keep Carla on staff, even though her performance is marginal? Should I add a new sales rep to help us grow? Would it make sense to cut a team member out of the accounting department to reduce our overhead? Should I honor Richard's request to work part time, so that he can go back to school?" It's not just those times when a job ad is posted that decision makers have to call the shots about hiring. By gaining a better understanding of what it's like to be in a hiring manager's shoes, you can begin to think more strategically about how to present yourself as a possible candidate. Small steps—like taking the initiative to contact a hiring manager *before* a position is advertised (the timing could be just right!), requesting a chance to introduce yourself to the manager, and following up multiple times to remind the decision maker of your interest—place you far ahead of the competition, while greatly increasing your chances for landing the best career opportunities.

Career Champ Profile: Ian

The architectural firm Ian worked for was relocating to another state. He could follow them if he wanted, and keep his job, but Ian really didn't want to move. He contacted Lance, a colleague at another firm, and asked if they could meet. Over coffee, Ian did a great job of describing his strengths and what he was looking for in his next job. He also showed Lance a list of architectural companies he was researching.

Lance knew the local architectural industry well and was able to provide Ian with names of nine other people to contact for network-ing. Lance also talked to Joan, his boss, about meeting Ian, in case they needed to add another architect to their team in the near future. Joan agreed to meet with Ian.

Before their interview, Ian talked again with Lance, studied the firm's Web site, and googled articles on the Internet to learn more about Joan's company and the projects they were working on. When he walked into the interview the following week, Ian took with him a resume emphasizing his relevant experience and a port-folio showcasing a few examples of his best work.

Joan asked him to describe specific instances in his background when he'd worked on projects similar to those her firm handled. Although he felt nervous, Ian responded with well-thought-out replies that demonstrated his expertise.

"Thanks for coming in today," Joan said, wrapping up the interview. "We may need to add another architect to the team, and it's great to know about your background." Ian thanked her for her time and interest and offered to provide her with any additional information she might need.

Later that day, Ian wrote and mailed a thoughtful thank-you note. A week later, Joan called requesting a second meeting. At the meeting, Joan pushed a box across the table to Ian. "Open it," she urged. Inside Ian found a supply of business cards, imprinted with the logo for Joan's firm and his name. "I was having some business cards printed anyway, and I took a chance that you might want a job here. Would you?" she asked.

Ian was excited, but managed to stay level-headed as they talked through the details of the offer. Having recently researched his worth through salary information he'd obtained from his professional association and through an informal survey of colleagues, Ian had a clear idea of the compensation package he was seeking. Joan was able to come close to meeting his requirements.

"This all sounds great," Ian said, "and I'll need a little time to think about it. When do you need to hear back from me?" They agreed they'd talk again in two days, on Thursday.

During that third meeting, Ian requested an additional $2,000 in salary, plus a performance bonus that would benefit both himself and Joan's firm. Joan readily agreed to Ian's requests, and they set a start date. Ian was thrilled: He'd managed to land a great job with better pay without having to move.

Core Courage Concept

Decision makers are faced with hiring choices every day—not just when a help-wanted ad is posted. Learning about the hiring process from the decision maker's perspective allows you to see and respond to opportunities that other job searchers may miss. Yes, it may mean doing things differently from the average job hunter (and feel a little riskier, too), but the payoff potential will be so much greater.

Confidence Checklist

☐ Learn more about the hiring difficulties decision makers face—as well as ways that you can help make the process easier—and you'll achieve more successful interviewing results.

Chapter 3

Land More Interviews

Few things in life can produce as much anxiety as waiting for a phone call. Whether it's from your doctor with results of a test, from a love interest whom you're hoping to date, or from an employer you're hoping to interview with, playing "The Waiting Game" is maddening.

At least with job interviews (as compared to calls from your doctor or from your honey), you have *some* control over moving things forward. Unless a job ad specifically says, "No calls please," you have the option to check in on the status of your application. Although it might seem like a scary step to take, following up can *double* the rate of interviews you land. In this situation, a little courage can make a big difference.

Risk It or Run From It?

- **Risk Rating:** Low to medium.

- **Payoff Potential:** Big. Following up can significantly increase the number of interviews you land.

- **Time to Complete:** 2–10 minutes per follow-up attempt.

(continued)

(continued)

- **Bailout Strategy:** You don't have to follow up—most people don't. But if you want to increase your interview rate by as much as 50 percent, it's worth a try.

- **The "20 Percent Extra" Edge:** Write a script for what you want to say, and practice it. When you actually get a decision maker on the phone, you'll sound like you really have your act together.

- **"Go For It!" Bonus Activity:** Use a "Three strikes, you're out" approach to follow-up. Don't give up after the first try. Vary your follow-up methods between e-mail and phone calls. On your third attempt, give the decision maker a graceful out.

How to Land More Interviews

The following sections present some effective steps you can take to get more interviews in the pipeline.

Use E-mail and Voice Mail to Make Follow-up Seem Less Intimidating

Most job searchers use the "hit-and-run" approach to applying for jobs. They send in a resume and cover letter (that's the hit) and then run away, making no further contact at all with the employer. "They'll call me if they want me," they figure. Plus, it feels much safer to not follow up than to risk the chance of being rejected.

Yet following up on the applications you submit can significantly increase the number of interviews you land. The ideal situation is to find a way to follow up that doesn't seem overly scary to you. E-mail and voice mail offer two ideal avenues for accomplishing this.

E-mail can be sent anytime, day or night, with no chance of having to talk to the decision maker directly. Later, when the decision maker responds, you can take your time planning your next move without the pressure of having to react immediately.

Similarly, voice-mail messages can be left outside of regular business hours (before 7:00 a.m. or after 7:00 p.m.) with little risk of having the decision maker pick up the phone. With either approach, the following script helps move things forward:

> "I am following up on a resume I submitted for the [JOB TITLE] position you currently have open. This position appears to be a great match for my skills and background. I want to confirm that my materials have been received, and to find out what happens from here.

> "You can contact me at [E-MAIL OR PHONE]. If I haven't heard from you in the next day or so, I will follow up with you to make sure this message was received successfully. I look forward to talking with you soon."

Whichever method you choose—voice mail or e-mail—I guarantee that you'll immediately feel proud of yourself for taking a valuable step toward realizing your career goals.

Research the Best Person to Follow Up With

So who do you follow up with? Someone in the human resources department? Although a contact in HR can seem like the logical choice, think again. HR specialists are often in charge of organizing a search; however, they're usually not responsible for making hiring decisions. Instead, they act as gatekeepers earlier in the hiring process, and permit applicants to move forward only if they meet very rigid criteria. Follow up with an HR rep, and you're very likely to hear, "Don't call us. We'll call you."

Smarter job searchers find ways around HR. Typically, the decision maker in charge of the position is the best person to contact. To identify this person, ask yourself, "To whom would I be reporting?" It will probably be a department head or general manager. Find out that person's name through one of the following avenues:

- Research them on the company Web site.

- Look up the information in a business directory (check out resources at the reference desk of your local library).

- Call the receptionist and ask, "Who is in charge of the X department at your company?" When you're given a name, confirm the spelling and ask for an e-mail address, also.

Follow a Script so that You Know Exactly What to Say

The script in the preceding section will get you started. You should also have a response written and practiced for "Tell me about yourself" (see chapter 8). Frequently, decision makers break the ice in a conversation by asking this question.

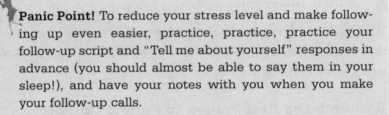

Panic Point! To reduce your stress level and make following up even easier, practice, practice, practice your follow-up script and "Tell me about yourself" responses in advance (you should almost be able to say them in your sleep!), and have your notes with you when you make your follow-up calls.

Have your calendar handy, too. Remember, your goal is to set an interview appointment—not to be interviewed on the phone! If the interviewer begins asking you several job-interview–type questions, move things forward by saying something like this:

"I would love to talk with you further about this position, but I need to leave for an appointment in a minute. I could meet with you tomorrow or Thursday. Would one of those days work for you, or should we choose another day?"

Motivate Yourself with Incentives to Overcome Your Fear and Actually Follow Up

Taking the step to make a phone call, leave a voice mail, or send an e-mail follow-up can seem overwhelming. So you'll need to pump yourself up or motivate yourself to actually make it happen. These techniques have worked for others:

- Write a list of three reasons why you should have a better job. Read the list to yourself before following up. Then say to yourself, "I'm doing this for myself to get what I deserve." Then do it.

- Give yourself a one-minute deadline to make your move. Pull out your watch and get started… the clock is ticking….

- Promise yourself a reward if you make one (or two, or five…) follow-up attempts. Choose a reward that's motivating for you: M&Ms, a latte, or a call to a friend to report your progress… it's up to you.

Use a "Three Strikes" Strategy

Keep a record of the applications you submit, and employ a clear-cut, "three strikes, you're out" strategy for multiple follow-up attempts. Set up a record-keeping system so that you'll know when you need to make your next follow-up move:

- **Strike 1** (Two to four days after you've submitted your resume): Voice mail or e-mail with the script from the preceding section.

- **Strike 2** (24 to 48 hours later): Voice mail or e-mail (you might want to vary your approach to keep it interesting) with the following message, "Just checking back on my message from yesterday. You can contact me at [PHONE or E-MAIL], or I'll try you again in a day or so."

- **Strike 3** (48 to 72 hours after that): Leave the following voice-mail message:

  "We seem to be having a hard time connecting, but I wanted to try reaching you one more time. I would very much like to talk to you about the [JOB TITLE] position you currently have open. I can be reached at [YOUR CONTACT INFO], and I'm hopeful I'll hear from you soon. Whether we get to talk or not, I wish you the best in finding the right person for this opportunity." (This is a classy way to let them off the hook if for some reason they can't, or won't, call you back.)

Why It's Worth Doing

When it comes to hiring, most employers are pretty disorganized. In fact, 75 percent of us work at companies with fewer than 25 employees, so there's no HR department to orchestrate an orderly, effective hiring process.

When a company does finally advertise a job, it's often because management is so overwhelmed that they're desperate for help. But that's just the start of the problem for them: After they run a job ad, and the applications start rolling in, they've got to figure out which candidates to interview. "How do I know which ones to choose? What do I look for?" It can seem like too much to handle. Frequently, they put off doing anything at all until a clear next step presents itself.

That's where you come in. When the overwhelmed decision maker receives a follow-up call from you, confirming that your application has been received and asking about the next step in the process, it tells him or her important information about you: You take initiative, you're organized, and you're confident enough to follow up (well, at least that's how it will look from the employer's perspective).

It also makes the next step easier for the decision maker. Since he's got you on the line, why not set up an interview?

Yes, it's a little scary to follow up. You risk the possibility of hearing, "No, we don't want to interview you." And that might be what you'll hear. But you also increase (by about 50 percent!) the chance of hearing, "How about if we schedule a time to interview you?"

Career Champ Profile: Joan

Joan had been job searching for an office manager job for months. A natural record keeper, she'd kept track of when she submitted applications, and regularly reviewed the status of each attempt. One day she realized that it had been three weeks since she'd responded to an ad for an office manager at a real-estate company. "I haven't heard anything from them. Maybe I should call…" Joan decided.

Joan was nervous about following up, but she pulled out a script, practiced it to herself a few times, told herself that she could call a friend as a reward after she'd made her follow-up call, took a deep breath, and dialed the number.

A woman answered on the third ring. Joan asked to speak with the person in charge of hiring the new office manager. The woman responded, "I'm Lara, the current office manager. Did you apply for the job?" Joan told her yes, and the woman continued: "I'm so glad you called. Gerry, my boss, has about 50 resumes in a pile on his desk. They've been sitting there for weeks, and he's done nothing with them at all. And tomorrow is my last day!"

The office manager put Joan through to Gerry. "Hi, Gerry," Joan began, reading her script. "I'm following up on your advertisement for an office manager. I submitted my resume a few weeks ago, and I want to make sure you received it okay."

"It's probably in this big stack on my desk," Gerry explained, "but I don't feel like digging through it right now. Could you bring another copy and meet with me sometime this afternoon?"

They set a time and Joan interviewed for the job, providing several examples of times when she'd successfully managed challenges like those in Gerry's office. "You're perfect," he said, and offered Joan the position. She began her training the next day with Lara, the office manager who was leaving.

"If you hadn't followed up, I don't know what would have happened," Lara said. Joan was glad she'd followed up, too.

Core Courage Concept

Following up is a small step than can make a huge difference in your results. Keep in mind that by following up on an application you've submitted, you help yourself get a job that will be a much better fit for you. Pushing through a few minutes of anxiety is a worthwhile tradeoff for creating a better career future.

Confidence Checklist

☐ Use e-mail and voice mail to make follow-up seem less intim-idating.

☐ Follow a script so that you know exactly what to say.

☐ Find out the best person to follow up with (Hint: It's not Human Resources).

☐ Motivate yourself with incentives to push through your fear and actually follow up.

☐ Keep a record of the applications you submit, so that you can time your follow-up attempts effectively.

☐ Employ a clear-cut, "Three strikes, you're out" strategy for multiple follow-up attempts.

Chapter 4

Plan Your Fearless Interview Strategy

For most of us, our biggest interviewing challenge is having enough belief in ourselves. Can we *really* do the job? Any doubt we feel comes through in the interview, making it difficult to present ourselves successfully.

There are ways to overcome this challenge, however. By simply gathering evidence about your experiences—evidence that is most likely sitting in your memory banks waiting to be recollected—you can build your belief in yourself and significantly improve your results in interviews.

Risk It or Run From It?

- **Risk Rating:** Zilch to very slight (you might experience a minor reality check).

- **Payoff Potential:** MASSIVE! If you do one step in this entire book, make it this one.

- **Time to Complete:** 30–90 minutes.

- **Bailout Strategy:** Don't even think about not doing this one! (Okay, if for some bizarre reason you do decide to skip

(continued)

(continued)

this step, at least spend some time thinking through your answers to the questions in chapters 8 and 9. Oh, and FYI, coming up with answers to those questions will be much easier for you if you complete this chapter first.)

- **The "20 Percent Extra" Edge:** Most people "intuitively" feel that they're a fit for a job—but they don't go through the steps to collect evidence that proves it. Then they hope their intuition will rescue them from a lack of preparation in an interview (it usually doesn't). After you go through the steps in this chapter, you'll be able to provide hard evidence that you are a fit for the job you want.

- **"Go For It!" Bonus Activity:** Put the valuable info you develop in this chapter into a Success Database that you can access in the future. You'll thank yourself many times over if you do.

How to Plan Your Fearless Interview Strategy

Follow these steps to prepare for a fearless interview experience.

Identify the Key Skill Areas for the Job

A solid (and fearless) interview strategy begins with an analysis of the key skills needed for the job. Typically, major clues about the crucial responsibilities for a position are included in the job ad. Let's say, for instance, that you applied in response to the following ad and have been contacted for an interview:

Cruise Reviewer Needed: *Experienced Cruiser* magazine seeks specialist to travel on one two-week cruise each month, experiencing all the food, services, and entertainment options the cruise has to offer. You will be expected to keep records of your impressions and experiences, based on our established review procedures. Within two weeks of completing the cruise, you will need to prepare a 2,000-word summary of your experiences and e-mail your report to company headquarters. Attractive pay and benefits package offered.

What would you say are the most important aspects of this job? Ask yourself, "In this position, what three to five tasks would I spend most of my time doing, and what skills would I use to execute those tasks well?" For instance:

- Task 1: Traveling on cruises and experiencing the amenities.

  Skill(s) Needed: Ability to travel 50 percent of the time, and willingness to explore a variety of foods and activities.

- Task 2: Keep records based on established procedures.

  Skill(s) Needed: Recordkeeping; ability to follow set procedures.

- Task 3: Write summaries.

  Skill(s) Needed: Analyzing information and writing.

- Task 4: E-mailing reports.

  Skill(s) Needed: Knowledge of computers.

Aim to identify the three to five most important responsibilities for the position. Usually you can pick these out simply by reading the job ad. If there's no job ad available, research ads for similar positions on a job search site such as www.monster.com. Search using keywords or a similar title (don't worry about geography—you're just looking for examples) and look for the key skills mentioned in those ads.

A government job information site, such as www.acinet.org, may also provide key skill information. Or you can contact the employer's hiring manager or human resources representative for details about the job responsibilities.

If none of these options is available to you—no job description, no similar position ads, no details from a company representative—then guess your best to identify the top three to five skills. Don't sweat coming up with the "perfect" skills list; the process allows for some wiggle room. By the way, from now on we'll be referring to these skills as the *key skill areas*.

Write your key skills on the following lines:

1. _____

2. _____

3. _____

4. _____

5. _____

Brainstorm Examples from Your Background that Demonstrate Your Expertise in Those Key Skill Areas

This is *the* most important step for convincing yourself that you're a great fit for the job (and consequently, the most crucial activity for transforming yourself from a Career Coward to a Career Champ in an interview!).

Brainstorm experiences from your background that are relevant to the job. If you can review the following information as you work through this exercise, it will make this step easier:

- Resumes (current and earlier versions)

- Performance reviews

- Letters of appreciation and congratulations from your supporters

- Any other resources that provide evidence about your experience and expertise, such as progress reports and school transcripts

Now look at the key skill areas list you developed in the first step and pick one skill area with which to start. I recommend choosing a skill area that seems easier to you, to get the process going successfully.

Let's take one of the key skill areas from the cruise reviewer job as an example:

Task 2: Keep records based on established procedures.

Skill(s) Needed: Recordkeeping; ability to follow set procedures.

Now ask yourself, "When have I demonstrated my expertise with recordkeeping and following procedures?" It might have come from a time when you were

- Working in a job.

- Completing a training or degree program.

- Involved in a volunteer project.

- Taking on a self-study project to learn and accomplish something you wanted to do.

Panic Point! At first you might think, "I have no experience doing that!" This is a common reaction, so don't panic. Take a deep breath and pull out your resume or school transcript. Now walk yourself through your history, asking yourself, "Have I ever kept records or followed procedures here? Or there?" Chances are, ideas will begin to come to you. "Oh, I did some recordkeeping on that job. And following procedures was pretty important when I worked there...." As you think of instances that provide evidence of your experience in a particular area, write them down. Even if they seem small and unimportant, add them to your list.

I've discovered that one of the primary roadblocks to building interview confidence is the candidate feeling that his or her experience isn't important or valuable enough. The Career Coward frequently worries that his examples will seem stupid or insignificant. This is a big mistake. Usually, hiring managers aren't looking for Wonder Worker Willie. They want Solid Performer Pete and Really Reliable

Reba. They don't need to hear that you changed the rotation of the Earth. They want to hear that you can handle day-to-day (seemingly insignificant) tasks well. So the example that might seem small or unimportant to you might be just the kind of example the decision maker is hoping to hear about. No matter how small your example may seem—especially at this stage of the process—write it down. (If you can come up with flashier, more impressive examples, list those too. But don't feel as if you *have* to.)

As you create your list of examples of times when you demonstrated your expertise in a particular key skill area, aim to come up with at least five. Why five? Because, typically, when you force yourself to brainstorm more than one or two, your last examples will be the best ones. It's as if your brain decides, "Okay, fine. Didn't like the first two I gave you? Try *these* on for size!"

For instance, as I brainstorm examples of recordkeeping and following procedures (because that cruise reviewer job sounds pretty good to me...), I come up with these:

- Example 1: Each week, I help with a volunteer coordination project at my church. It involves keeping records for what volunteer needs exist, and which volunteers can serve.

- Example 2: As a mom running a household, I keep financial and health records for the members of my family.

- Example 3: For several years, I've had to keep records on clients. I have to gather key pieces of information about them and store them correctly so that they can be accessed and used to help the client achieve his or her career goals.

- Example 4: Years ago, I worked at a law office copying one of the attorney's files. I had to follow strict procedures for checking files in and out of the records room.

- Example 5: While I was in graduate school, I worked on several detailed research projects that required me to both follow strict procedures and keep accurate records.

As you can see, I've brainstormed examples from many parts of my life: work, school, volunteer, and personal. At this stage in the process, they all count.

Now you can make your own list of examples that are relevant to a key skill area for your target job. When you've come up with five instances, move on to the next key skill area and brainstorm examples for that topic. Here are a few more tips that might help you with this part:

- Don't criticize your ideas now. Later, you'll have the opportunity to prioritize and choose your best examples.

- If you tell yourself, "This is a stupid idea," your brain will go on strike and stop giving you any more. Instead, say, "Okay, that's one. How about another?"

- If you get stuck and can't think of any examples at all, enlist the support of someone who knows and believes in you. Ask them to help you brainstorm instances when you demonstrated expertise in a particular skill area. Often, two heads are better than one.

- If you *really* get stuck, move on to the next key skill area and come back to the tough one later. You might be able to come up with some ideas then.

- It's okay to reuse a particular example for two or more key skill areas. For instance, I could use the graduate school example, "worked on several detailed research projects" as evidence of both my ability to keep records *and* to write summaries.

Key Skill Area 1:

1. _____

2. _____

3. _____

4. _____

5. _____

(continued)

(continued)

Key Skill Area 2:

1. _____

2. _____

3. _____

4. _____

5. _____

Key Skill Area 3:

1. _____

2. _____

3. _____

4. _____

5. _____

Key Skill Area 4:

1. _____

2. _____

3. _____

4. _____

5. _____

Key Skill Area 5:

1. _____

2. _____

3. _____

4. _____

5. _____

At the end of this step, you will have created a list of somewhere between 15 and 25 examples. Take time now to do a happy dance, call a friend, or eat an M&M—whatever activity signifies "Celebration!" to you. You've just completed a VERY BIG AND IMPORTANT STEP. Congratulations!

Why It's Worth Doing

Identifying the position's key skill areas gives you a focus for your interview preparation. When you know what these skills are, you can begin to collect evidence that shows you're a great fit. And the more evidence you collect, the more confident you'll be in presenting yourself in the interview!

Career Champ Profile: Jaynee

Jaynee had a job selling tickets at the dog track. Through a friend of a friend, she'd landed an interview at a bank for a position as a Teller Trainer. These were the key skill areas that were listed for the job:

- Key skill area 1: Assess skill-development needs for new and existing tellers.

- Key skill area 2: Develop or identify training resources to meet those needs.

- Key skill area 3: Lead group and individual training sessions as needed.

"I'm terrified," Jaynee told me when we met to prepare. "I'd love to have this job, and I think I could do it...but how do I prove it to them? I'm just a ticket clerk at the dog track!"

I asked her to tell me about her current work. "I go to work. I check out my drawer from the accountant at the track. I sell tickets. I balance my drawer. I return my drawer to the accountant. I go home."

I confess: At first it sounded as if she had very little related experience, and I caught myself thinking, "Yikes...this is going to be a long shot!" But I quickly reminded myself that fantastic experiences often lie beneath the surface of a person's current work. It turned out I was right.

"Let's take this one key skill area at a time," I said. "First, tell me about any background you have assessing skill-development needs for tellers."

Jaynee then told me that she worked as a teller once for two years. "I was pretty good at it. My drawer always balanced." She told me that she'd also worked at a manufacturing company as Shift Trainer. "Every time someone new was hired, I worked with them to get them up to speed on the task they were assigned to do. I showed them the process, I watched them do it themselves, and then I identified areas where they needed to improve and helped them in those areas." I was beginning to feel more optimistic about Jaynee's chances.

"Now tell me about any experience you have in developing or identifying training resources." Jaynee then rattled off three examples of times when she'd done that kind of work. This was one of them: "In my current job at the track, I put together a training program for new ticket sellers. I could see there was a need for it because every time someone new was hired, my boss would put them on the ticket line with just a few minutes of training. Within an hour or two, they'd start making mistakes and asking the other ticket sellers lots of questions.

"I figured it would be better for everyone if there was a standard training process. So I asked my boss if I could develop one. He said 'Yes,' so I did it. I analyzed all the steps in the process, including several 'What if this happens?' scenarios. I wrote up the procedures, ran them by my boss, and tested them with the next new hire on the line.

"It worked great. The training now takes half a day—so it's longer than it used to be—but the last new hire that got trained rarely asks questions and she still hasn't made any major mistakes in the three months she's worked there."

Jaynee's relevant experiences were really shaping up nicely. "Okay, skill area 3: Leading group and individual training sessions. What can you tell me about your qualifications in that area?"

As she'd already mentioned, Jaynee had done one-on-one training with manufacturing workers and new hires at the track. But what about training to groups? "I did train groups at the manufacturing company. Each quarter we had a safety unit that we had to go over with the shift workers. There was even a test they had to take at the end, proving that they'd understood the information successfully. Of the four shift trainers at the company, the groups I trained consistently received the highest grades on the tests. I guess that shows I was an effective group trainer, right?"

Jaynee continued to share examples of her relevant experience, and soon we had a long list of examples to work with. I could see her confidence grow with every example we added to her list.

A few days later, fully prepared, Jaynee walked into the interview feeling very confident about her fit for the job. And in the end, she received an offer!

Core Courage Concept

Analyzing what you *truly* have to offer to an employer is scary. What if it turns out you don't have enough of the right stuff? Yet when you do take the time to think through your experiences, asking yourself, "Have I done this before?" the answer will usually be yes — and *you* will have the evidence to prove it!

Confidence Checklist

☐ Identify the key skill areas for the job you want.

☐ Brainstorm examples from your background that demonstrate your expertise in those key skill areas.

Chapter 5

Put Muscle into Your Interviewing Plan

I n interviews, it's not unusual to be at a loss for words — especially when it comes to promoting yourself. "Arrgh! What should I say? I don't want to sound like a conceited, self-focused idiot!" you might worry. So how *do* you promote yourself successfully without sounding like you're bragging?

By creating a collection of What, How, and Proof stories that describe your accomplishments, you arm yourself with interview responses that deliver convincing facts *and* entertaining self-promotion — with this delightful bonus: The more evidence you collect, the more confident you'll feel about yourself!

Risk It or Run From It?

- **Risk Rating:** Low. You'll only need to think and write.

- **Payoff Potential:** Significant. Every minute you spend on this activity will further build your belief in yourself as a top-notch candidate.

- **Time to Complete:** 30 minutes to a few hours.

(continued)

(continued)

- **Bailout Strategy:** You can rely on what you developed in chapter 4. But if want to build your courage further, work through this chapter, too.

- **The "20 Percent Extra" Edge:** Thinking through "What, How, and Proof" statements saves you from the panic of thinking "Oh no! What will I say?" in front of a decision maker.

- **"Go For It!" Bonus Activity:** Create a typed, one-page list of your most impressive examples and share this success document with the hiring manager during the interview.

How to Put Some Muscle into Your Interviewing Plan

The following six steps will help you ramp up your interviewing strategy and bring it one step closer to reality.

Learn the "What, How, and Proof" Process

In chapter 4, you produced evidence that yes, you can succeed in a particular key skill area. Now you'll develop those examples into compelling stories that will allow you to successfully and courageously promote yourself in an interview. So when you're asked, "Tell me about your experience in…," you'll be ready with a great answer.

For this part of the process, you'll use the foolproof "What, How, and Proof" format:

- **What:** *What* was going on? What happened to cause you to become involved in this activity? What problem needed to be solved, or what plan needed to be implemented?

- **How:** *How* did you handle the situation? What did you do first, next, and so on, to get the job done? Provide a step-by-step account of your actions, even if it seems like way too much detail. You can edit out some of the finer points later.

- **Proof:** What *proof* do you have that your efforts paid off? Did you

  1. Save money?

  2. Make money?

  3. Improve quality?

  4. Improve the organization's image?

  What were the results?

Here's an example of a What, How, and Proof story using one of the examples I developed for "keeping records and following procedures" in chapter 4:

Original example:

> "For several years, I've kept client records. I have to gather key pieces of information about them and store them correctly so that they can be accessed and used to help the client achieve his or her career goals."

Now here's that example developed into a What, How, and Proof story:

- **What:** As a counselor, a big part of my work has been collecting and keeping records on about 2,000 clients. This is important because this data helps me assist clients in improving their career situations.

- **How:** I use several methods to effectively collect and store client information: I interview clients and take notes on what they say, and I give them assessments and write up the results. Then I store this information in client files, as well as in a Microsoft Access database. I use forms and checklists to make sure I'm being consistent and following the established procedures. Each week I have about 30 client meetings, so that turns out to be about 1,500 instances each year when I need to keep records according to the procedures.

- **Proof:** I know that I am a successful record-keeper because there have been only four times in the last eight years when a record was incorrect or missing—out of over 10,000 record-keeping sessions! This contributes to the company's positive image for delivering a quality service and has helped the business grow by about 20 percent per year for the last six years.

Now, imagine that you're a hiring manager looking for someone with recordkeeping skills. You've asked the candidate, "Tell me about your recordkeeping experience." Would you rather hear the What, How, and Proof answer written above, or the average-Joe response listed below?

"I am a good record-keeper. I have kept records and followed procedures at several jobs in the past."

Zzzzzzzzzzzzzz.... (Oops, sorry. Fell asleep there....)

The What, How, and Proof story definitely has more impact!

Now it's your turn to develop some powerful What, How, and Proof stories of your own.

Pick a Key Skill Area Example and Describe the "What" of the Situation

Choose your example from the list you developed in chapter 4 and ask yourself, "What was going on in this situation? Was there a problem I needed to solve or a plan that I needed to implement?" Write a few notes about the circumstances.

Panic Point! If you haven't noticed yet, getting this part started is *hard*. Many people put the brakes on at this point. Don't let that be you! Push through the fear, confusion, or resistance you might be feeling and give this step a whirl. You will be SO PROUD of yourself after you've succeeded, I promise! To make this tough step a little easier, just write down a short phrase about what was happening at that time.

For instance, if I was describing the "What" of my lawyer's office recordkeeping example, I might write

"Lawyer was leaving law firm."

Good. It's a start. Now, a little more about what was going on:

"All his files needed to be copied."

And just a bit more detail:

"I was hired to copy all those files."

Enough!

What you write doesn't need to be perfectly worded. You just need to include enough details that paint a picture of the situation.

Got it? Good. Moving on…

Write a Few Sentences About "How" You Did It

This will probably be a little easier because it's like giving a blow-by-blow report of what you've done. Ask yourself, "What specific steps did I take to accomplish the task?" Aim to provide a step-by-step account of your process. Again, phrases are sufficient:

1. The office manager at the law firm showed me what needed to be copied.

2. There was a specific process for checking files in and out of the file room, and I could check out only one file at a time.

3. I copied each file page by page, front and back, keeping all the documents in the proper order.

4. After a file was copied, I had to check the original file and the copied file back into the file room, to maintain client confidentiality.

5. Altogether, there were over 1,500 files that I needed to copy over a three-month period.

That's it!

Describe the Results of What Happened—the "Proof" that You Did Well

Career Cowards tend to run and hide when they get to this step. But this is the final piece—don't quit now! Do it, and you'll learn how to hit a home run in an interview (and actually, it's not as scary as you fear it might be).

"But I really didn't have a positive result," you might be worrying. Fear not. If you did the work well, there's a worthwhile outcome to describe.

For instance, continuing with my law office example, I ask myself, "Did I help the organization

- Save money?" Well, yes! If the files hadn't been copied correctly, and if client confidentially had been breached, the law firm could have been sued, and that would have cost them a lot of money.

- Make money?" Did I add anything to the bottom line? No, I guess not. On to the next one...

- Improve quality?" Yes! Properly copied files support delivery of quality legal services. My quality copy job did support the ability of the law firm to provide successful services in the future.

- Improve image?" Yes! Helping the departing lawyer prepare for his next position maintained good professional relationships, contributing to the positive image of the firm.

Now it's your turn. Describing your result might feel frightening, but press on. We're just brainstorming. Use the "write just a short phrase" technique again to get started, answering these questions about one of your examples:

- How might I have saved the business money?

- How might I have made the business money?

- How might I have improved the business's quality?

- How might I have improved the business's image?

_____

_____

_____

_____

_____

_____

_____

_____

_____

How'd you do? Got a few small ideas? Great! You'll get better at this as you practice it more. Here are some additional ways to look at your results information:

- How many times did you do something? How many pieces did you process? In what timeframe? Remember, you don't need an _exact_ count. You're allowed to say, "Approximately...."

- What other departments/customers/people did you help, even if it was indirectly? What did you do for them?

- What impact did your work have on the long-term performance of the organization? Has the organization grown or thrived, due in part to your quality contributions?

- How did other people describe your work? Have they made positive comments? Did they note favorable things about you in your performance review? What did they say?

See if you can come up with a few more details to add to your results information. Keep in mind that this is your first What, How, and Proof story, so it's bound to be a little rough. Realize that you'll get better at this as you go along.

Put Your What, How, and Proof Pieces Together for a Real WOW! Experience

This is the fun part...plus, it's easy-sneezy! Just line up your What, How, and Proof information back to back:

- **What:** I worked at a law firm and a lawyer was leaving. All his files needed to be copied so that he could take a set with him to his new firm. I was hired to copy all those files.

- **How:** The office manager at the law firm showed me what needed to be copied. I had to follow a specific process for checking files in and out of the file room. I could check out only one file at a time. I copied each file page by page, front and back, keeping all the documents in the proper order. After a file was copied, I had to check the original file and the copied file back into the file room, to maintain client confidentiality. Altogether, I copied more than 1,500 files in just over three months.

- **Proof:** I know I did well with this job because I followed procedures carefully, maintaining client confidentiality and protecting the law firm from being sued. I also helped the firm continue to deliver quality legal services by copying files correctly. Another result of my quality record-keeping skills was that I helped the departing lawyer prepare for his next position, supporting good ongoing professional relationships between the two law firms and contributing to the positive image of the firm.

Okay, your turn. Put your What, How, and Proof pieces together and look at the result. Now read what you've written out loud. Sounds pretty good, huh? Let's do some more!

_____

_____

_____

_____

_____

_____

_____

_____

_____

_____

_____

_____

_____

_____

_____

Repeat This Process with More Key Skill Area Examples

You know the drill. Aim to create one What, How, and Proof story for each key skill area. Most likely, with each What, How, and Proof story you create, the process will get easier and you'll feel a bit more confident about your ability to promote your skills successfully in an interview.

Once you've created the first round of What, How, and Proof stories, challenge yourself to create another round—another one for each key skill area. Soon you will have created one of the most powerful self-promotion tools you'll ever have: A Success Database.

Enter all of your What, How, and Proof stories into a word-processing or spreadsheet file for easy access in the future. You'll be accessing them to help you answer some of those tough interview questions, such as "Tell me about yourself" and "What are your strengths and weaknesses?"

Finally, give yourself a pat on the back or some other reward. You've earned it!

Why It's Worth Doing

It can be difficult to promote yourself effectively in an interview. When you're nervous, you're lucky enough to remember your name, let alone some impressive details about your background. Learning how to create What, How, and Proof stories provides you with an effective, easy-to-remember method for sharing valuable information about yourself—a technique that you'll be able to remember even when you're stressed!

Career Champ Profile: Alex

Alex had been a Finance Manager for a county government for almost two decades and was ready to take his career to the next level. When a Chief Financial Officer position opened up with a government contract organization, he customized his resume and landed an interview.

"I've got a problem, though," he told me in our interview-prep session. "They want experience with negotiating coal and gas contracts, and I've never done that before."

I was determined to prove him wrong and to show him that yes, he did have relevant experience in that key skill area. "Do you have any experience negotiating contracts at all?" I asked him.

Alex told me that he'd negotiated hundreds of contracts, many of them to line up contractors for construction projects. "Anything to do with fuel?" I prompted. "Well, yes, I did negotiate electricity contracts for the county a few times." "Okay, what about coal or gas?" I asked, nudging him further. "Nothing I can think of with coal," he began, "but with gas, I attended a government financial managers' conference this year, and sat in on a presentation about structuring gas contracts. I'd forgotten about that! I even have the handouts from the presentation. *And*, I have the name of the presenter! I ended up sitting next to him during the lunch break, and we talked for a while. I could call him for some more tips about what I might need to know for this job." This provided a potential What, How, and

Proof story that Alex could use in response to questions about his gas contracts experience.

Alex also came up with this story about his background in contracts:

> "A few years ago, I could see that the county was going to face a budget deficit due to increases in electricity prices—increases that had been impossible for us to forecast the year before. I was motivated to minimize that deficit, so I got busy researching cheaper sources of electricity. Through an energy coop, I was able to get a lead on a bulk electricity purchase through a power broker. I researched competitive pricing and negotiated an energy purchase that resulted in a $200,000 savings to the county. That savings kept the county from going into the red that year."

With each What, How, and Proof statement he developed, Alex's anxiety shrank and his confidence grew. He was able to carry that belief in himself into the interview.

Core Courage Concept

Hiring managers want evidence that a candidate can do the job. What, How, and Proof stories provide that evidence. Although it can feel scary to put the hard facts about your abilities into words, once you do, you'll realize that there's great power in having the details at your fingertips. Sweating through the process of creating those stories now will save you from sweating (and failing) in an interview later.

Confidence Checklist

☐ Learn the "What, How, and Proof" process.

☐ Pick a key skill area example from the list you developed in chapter 4 and describe the "What" of the situation.

☐ Write a few sentences about "How" you did it.

☐ Describe the results of what happened—the "Proof" that you did well.

☐ Put your What, How, and Proof pieces together for a real "Wow! That's really me?!" experience.

☐ Repeat this process with more key skill area examples.

Chapter 6

Uncover Company Info to Increase Your Confidence

Every business and person is unique, each with distinct characteristics and priorities. By understanding the individual differences of the company and people with whom you're interviewing, you can present yourself more effectively and position yourself ahead of the competition.

Imagine, for instance, saying to the hiring manager, "I notice that your company recently introduced a service that addresses a new niche in the market," or "I did a little research on your main competitors, and you seem have an advantage based on the financing options you offer."

Uncovering key pieces of information—about the company, the industry, and its key players—allows you to build your interviewing confidence, while making you significantly more attractive to the hiring manager.

Risk It or Run From It?

- **Risk Rating:** Zero to very slight (if you choose to make a phone call or two).

(continued)

(continued)

- **Payoff Potential:** Definitely worth the effort. Most candidates don't do this step well, so here's an opportunity to set yourself apart.

- **Time to Complete:** 30 minutes to a couple of hours.

- **Bailout Strategy:** If you don't want to analyze the employer's needs (or can't for some reason), you can rely on the prep work you did in chapters 4 and 5. But you might miss out on some prime opportunities to solidify yourself as the top candidate.

- **The "20 Percent Extra" Edge:** Most candidates skim a company's Web site for a few minutes before an interview, gathering some basic information about the business and its services. Career Champs go deeper, spending a few hours researching recent company developments, the industry, the competition, and the key players.

- **"Go For It!" Bonus Activity:** Contact people in your network and ask them for any information they can offer about the company, decision makers, and so on.

How to Uncover Company Info

The following steps should garner you lots of very helpful inside information about the company you are interviewing with.

Research the Company and Key Employees

You've already analyzed your experience related to the position's key skill areas. Now here's your chance to view things from the other side of the table: What's going on from the employer's perspective? Related to the sample position from chapter 4, for instance, you could research *Experienced Cruiser* magazine.

Begin your sleuthing on the organization's Web site. Review its products, services, mission, and employee profiles. If they are available, read some sample articles.

Next, log onto a search engine and enter keywords such as "Experienced Cruiser magazine" for press releases and articles describing recent activities and involvements. Use quotation marks around multi-word phrases so that the search engine finds only the places where all these words appear together, in order. You can also enter into the search engine employee names, to get background info on key players. Seek out the following details:

- What are the company's most important products and services?

- Which customers do they serve, and what problems do they solve for them?

- Who heads the company/department in which you'd be working?

Finding even a little extra information about the company and people can give you an important edge. Use the people in your network as another source of information. Call or e-mail them with this message:

> Bob, next Monday I'm interviewing for a job at *Experienced Cruiser.* Julie Smith, Kyle Green, and Martha Gephardt are on the interview team. I'd like to gather as much information as possible about the company, their projects, and the team. Do you have any information to share, or could you recommend anybody I should contact who might know more?

Sometimes just one or two choice pieces of information can make a huge impact in an interview. Pete, a friend of mine, told me once how he and his team members had interviewed John, a potential employee, for an engineering position. Prior to the interview, John had checked out all the members of the interview team on a search engine, providing him with several conversation starters.

For instance, John had come across Pete's guitar Web site (Pete is an engineer by day and a Spanish guitarist on nights and weekends) and read about several of his performances. John mentioned his discovery to Pete in the interview. "The fact that John had done all that research really set him apart from the other candidates. It seemed as though he was able to connect with the team right away, and that was important to us. We ended up hiring him."

Collect all the company, product, and people information you uncover in your research, for use in the interview later.

Study the Industry and Competition

For an even greater understanding of the company, learn about the bigger picture of your potential employer's industry.

For instance, *Experienced Cruiser* magazine isn't the only cruising publication on the market. An online search with the keywords, "Cruise Magazine" would reveal several other players in the cruise publications industry, including several cruise Web sites, videos, and books. All of these information sources are competing for a cruiser's dollars, and are therefore competition for *Experienced Cruiser* magazine.

Spend some time analyzing your potential employer's competition. Who offers what? What are each supplier's strengths and weaknesses? Depending on the industry, this might seem like an overwhelming task. If the information seems daunting, consider enlisting the help of a research librarian to help you identify the primary rivals.

While you're researching competitors, seek out industry info, too. On your favorite search engine, enter keywords such as, "Cruise Industry Data," and aim to learn a little about

- The dollar value of the market
- Whether the market is growing or shrinking each year, and by how much
- What industry analysts have to say about key trends

Add that data to the info you've already gathered in your company profile, and you're ready to put together some key pieces for the final step.

Determine Opportunities to Emphasize Other Relevant Aspects of Your Experience

Let's say, for example, that a conversation with a colleague revealed that the former cruise reviewer was fired because she frequently missed her submission-review deadlines. Considering this, you'd want to provide information in the interview about your stellar ability to meet submission timelines.

You might have also discovered—through your industry research—that a trend in the cruise publishing industry is a movement toward e-mail delivery of review information customized to each subscriber's preferences. Any background you have in that area would be wise to mention as well.

Wrap any additional insights into your company profile and What, How, and Proof stories. Congratulations! You've already made huge progress toward building your confidence and performing successfully in your interview.

Why It's Worth Doing

Not knowing what to expect in interviews is one of the biggest sources of fear. That's why, in battle, military leaders put so much energy into researching and understanding the enemy. Knowing what to expect reduces anxiety and builds confidence. Learning about the company and its key players, competition, and industry gives you the understanding that leads to that confidence.

Remember the last time you felt really confused or scared? That kind of fear usually shows up at those times when you have very little information about what's going on. Questions fill your head, such as "What will happen next? Will I be okay? What do I need to plan for?"

For example, fear came up for me several times as my daughter moved further and further into her teens. Drugs, sex, rock 'n roll…you name it, it scared me.

After running into several frightening situations with her, I noticed a pattern was emerging: First, a new situation would pop up and I'd panic. Next, I'd feel confused and overwhelmed. Shortly thereafter I'd start to gather information about possible risks, talking to specialists and researching information on the Internet. As I gathered more information, my anxiety dropped. Eventually, rather than feel panicked, I began to feel a little like an expert. Even though I'd started off feeling overwhelmed, I wound up feeling as if I'd gained important new strategies and information—and was becoming more skilled as a parent!

The feelings and steps you'll go through in preparing for an interview will most likely follow a similar pattern: At first you'll feel overwhelmed. Then, you'll start to gather information. As pieces of the puzzle come together—what the job will entail, what the company does, who you would be working with, what's going on in the industry—you'll start to feel more confident about where you fit and how you can contribute.

Invest an hour or two in some research about the organization, and by the time you walk in the door for the interview, you'll feel as if you already know the place, the people, and their priorities. That information will build your belief in yourself that you are the best candidate for the position!

Career Champ Profile: Nina

Nina had been wilting in a job as a secretary at a university. Although she enjoyed using her strengths in organization and helping others, she really longed to use her interior design skills. Through a friend, Nina heard about an opening for an office manager at a window-coverings company, and landed a job interview. Nina saw it as a great opportunity to use her administrative skills in a business that was linked to the interior design industry—but the thought of interviewing for a position that excited her as much as this one did made her especially nervous.

To calm her anxiety and improve her performance, Nina decided to learn as much as she could about the job and the company before the interview. Through her friend, Nina was able to talk with the former office manager to find out what the job entailed. She also researched the firm and its lead designer on Google and through the company Web site. One link led her to a local newspaper article mentioning the firm's recent completion of a window-coverings project for the local opera house. Nina took a tour of the facility to get a closer look at the treatments.

Nina also looked up other window-treatment companies in the area, listed in the Yellow Pages section of her phone book. She looked at the competitors' Web sites, and even called a few of the places, posing as a potential customer, to learn about their services and products.

As a final preparation step, Nina researched the bookkeeping program the former office manager told her the firm used, and took an online tutorial to gain some basic knowledge. At the library, a business reference specialist helped Nina find information about recent developments in the window-coverings industry.

By the time Nina walked into the building for her interview, she felt as if she was already working there. Although she still felt a little nervous, she was mostly excited. At the start of the interview, Jillian, the firm's owner, asked Nina several standard interview questions, such as "Tell me about yourself," and "What are your strengths and weaknesses?" Nina responded with well-planned answers and felt great about how things were going.

Later in the interview, when Nina mentioned that she'd seen the new window treatments at the opera house, Jillian's interest in Nina increased immediately. "Tell me about your experience in bookkeeping," Jillian said. Nina told Jillian that she handled the budgeting and financial recordkeeping for her department at the college, and that she'd recently completed a tutorial of DesignBooks, the bookkeeping system Jillian's firm used. "It's pretty similar to the program I use at the university," Nina explained.

Jillian was visibly excited and impressed with Nina. "You come highly recommended," Jillian told her. "I'll be making a decision next week, and I'll definitely be calling you."

Nina left feeling more pleased with her interview performance than she'd ever been before. A little extra time and effort invested in researching her potential employer had made a huge difference in her confidence and performance.

Core Courage Concept

It takes time and effort to research a company before the interview. But the payoff is greatly increased confidence and the ability to significantly improve your performance. A little extra effort on the front end can lead to big payoffs in the interview.

Confidence Checklist

☐ Research the company and key employees.

☐ Study the industry and the company's competition.

☐ Determine opportunities to emphasize other relevant aspects of your experience.

Chapter 7

Polish Your Best Interviewing Tools

Think about your favorite cooking utensils in the kitchen. You know...the wooden spoon you always reach for, or the bowl you always use for your cereal. You choose these items because they're familiar to you, and you know they'll help you get the job done.

In an interview, you want your What, How, and Proof stories to be as comfortable and helpful to you as your favorite wooden spoon. But just as it took you several uses to learn that your wooden spoon was reliable and capable, it will take you several practice sessions to develop a successful familiarity with your stories. This chapter will lead you through that valuable process of practicing.

Risk It or Run From It?

- **Risk Rating:** Technically, zip. But as you practice, it might make your heart pump a little faster.

- **Payoff Potential:** Well, considering that practice makes perfect, and if you're hoping for a close-to-perfection performance, the payoff could be significant.

(continued)

(continued)

- **Time to Complete:** That's your call—a little or a lot. More is better.

- **Bailout Strategy:** If you have a photographic memory and can recall the What, How, and Proof statements you've already developed—and if you're gifted at telling compelling stories with very little practice, maybe you could skip this step. But as the true greats of the world have proven, the more you work at something, the better you get.

- **The "20 Percent Extra" Edge:** Practice builds polish. Putting in the time and effort to smooth the rough edges of your delivery will pay off with a much better performance.

- **"Go For It!" Bonus Activity:** Record or videotape your practice. Hearing and watching how you come across to others is effective in showing you where you still need to improve.

How to Polish Your Interviewing Tools

Here are some ways to dip your toe into the interviewing process and build up skills that will help you later.

Learn a Little About Interviews

In three words, describe your last interview experience: Tough? Disorganized? Fun? Structured? Exhausting? Bizarre? Terrific? Dreadful? There are as many styles of interviews as there are personalities of hiring managers. It might be a well-organized event, a thrown-together circus act, or something in between.

As a general guideline, the bigger the company, the more organized the interview process will be. Larger businesses typically have more structured systems for hiring, complete with human resources departments, defined hiring processes, and training sessions that teach managers which questions to ask to evaluate a candidate's worth.

Yet 75 percent of us work at companies with fewer than 25 employees. That means that the vast majority of interviews happen at small businesses — and more often than not, the interview process is disorganized. It's not unusual, for instance, for a candidate to show up at a small-company interview to be greeted by a hiring manager who says, "Oh, yes! I'm interviewing you today. Let's see, where shall we start?" Often, they put no time into preparing.

Panic Point! Does this make you even more nervous? Don't be. If they're disorganized and you're prepared, you'll be able to guide the conversation successfully. And if they're organized, you'll be ready for that, too.

Practicing and polishing your What, How, and Proof stories will give you the tools to handle any kind of interview situation successfully. You've already done the tough work of analyzing the position's key skill areas and developing your What, How, and Proof stories (hooray for you!!). Now you'll polish them into shining interview responses that you'll feel confident and proud to share.

Try Your Hand at a Rough Run-Through

Find a place where you can talk out loud to yourself without feeling like a goofball. If you live in a busy house, this can be a challenge. One time I needed to find a place to verbally practice a presentation, and there was no private place in my house. So I ended up practicing while I mowed the lawn! My family couldn't hear what I was saying over the roar of the lawnmower, so it worked for me (yet I wonder what the neighbors were thinking…). Other private-place options include

- In your car at a park

- In your car while driving somewhere (people will think you're talking on a hands-free cell phone)

- A borrowed room at your office or place of worship during off hours

Wherever you decide to practice, take along the following:

- Your What, How, and Proof stories

- A pencil, highlighter, and notepaper

- A timing device (such as a stopwatch or a timepiece with a second hand)

- Optional: A recording device (audio or video) if you want to hear how you're coming across

To begin, pull out one of your favorite stories and pretend that an interviewer has asked you the following:

> Tell me about a time when you demonstrated your expertise in (fill in the key skill area, such as "record-keeping").

Start your timer and then read through your story. Read it just as you've written it, with no modifications. Read it at a reasonable pace—not too fast, not too slowly, as if you were talking with a 10-year-old. (10-year-olds can comprehend most things as long as you don't talk too fast!) When you're finished, write down the length of time it took for you to read it.

You might be feeling like you want to change some things in your story now that you've read it out loud. That's okay, and we'll get to that part soon. For now, you're just getting used to the sound of your voice and timing how long it takes to read each story.

Move on to the next story, reading through and timing that one— and then the next one, and the next one, until you've read them all. Now we'll refine your delivery a bit.

Practice a Few More Times, with Some Minor Changes

Go back to your favorite story. How long did it take you to read it? Ideally, you want the length of your stories to be between one and two minutes. If it's longer than that (and it probably is—most What, How, and Proof stories start off being pretty long), you'll want to trim it down a bit.

To do that, work through your first What, How, and Proof story again, making these adjustments:

- Rewrite any parts of your story that seemed awkward or too long when you read through it the first time.

- Ask yourself, "If someone who doesn't know anything about my background or the situation heard this story, would they understand enough of what I'm talking about to get the basic gist of things?" If the answer is no, go back and make some additional edits to make things more clear.

- Highlight the most important parts of the story—the key phrases that describe what happened, how you responded to the challenge, and the proof that it worked well—to make sure that those parts get priority attention as you practice.

Now read through the story again, timing it to check its length. How did you do? More changes needed? Make any necessary revisions.

Attain "Good Enough!"

Read through your stories over and over until they start to feel like a pair of your favorite shoes: comfortable and able to help you get to where you want to go. Your goal is to reach a point where you can

- Tell the story without forgetting any major points.

- Convey it within a reasonable one- to two-minute timeframe.

- Communicate the details clearly and without feeling overly stressed.

When you've reached that point, you've attained the "good enough" stage. Congratulations! You've just polished some of your most valuable interview tools. Already, you're miles ahead of your interviewing competition.

Why It's Worth Doing

Under stress (and as you know, interviews can be very stressful), we resort to what we know best—even though it might not show us at our best. For instance, if you were asked, "Tell us about your experience working on computers," you might blurt out, "I really get nervous learning new programs!" without even thinking about what you're saying.

By practicing and polishing your core What, How, and Proof stories, you create a toolbox of several excellent responses, ready to be pulled out as you need them. So when the next stressful, "Tell us about your experience working on computers," question comes your way, you can respond with, "Sure! Here's an example about my computer background...."

Practicing What, How, and Proof examples can mean the difference between a good performance in an interview and a *great* one.

Career Champ Profile: Josh

Josh was aiming for a position as a sales proposal coordinator. With an interview coming up, he'd identified the key skill areas for the job and developed a great set of What, How, and Proof stories as evidence of his expertise. Now he was in the initial practice phase, rehearsing and refining his stories. He'd been working on a few in the week since we'd last met, and now it was time to practice.

I began the mock interview: "Give me an example of a time when you demonstrated your expertise in the area of working with customers to gather information and solve problems." Josh broke eye contact with me, looking off to the side as he formulated his answer. "When I worked at the post office," he began slowly, "I had to set up and organize 1,900 post-office boxes...." His voice trailed off. "Also, I worked at a telemarketing firm once, surveying customers for information and answering product questions." His gaze returned to me.

"Okay, now tell me about a time when you had to pay attention to all of the details in a finished document," I asked him. "Oh, sure!" he started enthusiastically. "When I was in grad school, I took a computer technology class. The teacher gave us assignments that helped us learn and apply new skills using Microsoft Word, Access, Excel, and PowerPoint."

Josh continued, looking directly at me with his eyes shining in excitement. "Well, it turned out that there were mistakes in his assignments—mistakes that made it very difficult to complete the assignments correctly, or errors that made it possible for the student to slide through the assignment with very little effort, essentially learning nothing. After class one day, I pointed out a few of the errors to the instructor.

"The professor was so impressed with my attention to detail that he hired me to review and correct the entire 100-page assignments workbook. I did a great job with that project, and the professor kept me on as teaching assistant for more than three years, until I gradu-ated. The students who took the course over those next three years turned in assignments that showed a much higher level of learning, due in large part to a workbook that was accurate and thorough."

"Great story!" I congratulated Josh. But then it hit me how Josh's delivery of the two What, How, and Proof stories had been so dif-ferent. In the "gathering information from customers" story, Josh's phrasing had been slow and hesitant. He seemed visibly nervous and unsure of himself. In the second story, about the workbook, he was excited and confident. "What was the difference between those two for you?" I asked, hoping to solve the mystery.

Josh laughed. "That's easy," he replied. "I practiced the workbook story about five times since our last meeting. By now, I'm pretty comfortable telling that story. I didn't practice the other story at all—just wrote it down on paper. So I'm not as relaxed telling that one."

Over the next few days, Josh was able to practice each of his What, How, and Proof stories several times until he was able to tell each one with a similar level of comfort and excitement...and his efforts made a huge difference in the interview, allowing Josh to present himself as confident and effective rather than nervous and insecure.

Core Courage Concept

Practicing can be nerve-wracking. Your voice may sound weird, and will you ever *really* be able to come up with something that sounds impressive to the interviewer? Although it does sound weird to hear yourself talk, and although you probably won't be able to come up with the *perfect* interview response, working through the strangeness of practicing will go a long way toward boosting your confidence in your ability to say something brilliant at just the right time in an interview.

Confidence Checklist

- ☐ Learn a little about interviews.
- ☐ Try your hand at a rough run-through.
- ☐ Practice a few more times, with some minor changes.
- ☐ Attain "good enough!"

Chapter 8

Tell Me About You! (Strengths and Weaknesses, Too...)

"Tell me about yourself," "Describe your greatest strength," and "What are your weaknesses?" are some of the toughest questions interview candidates face. Your responses need to be truthful—but not so honest that you kill your chances of getting the job!

This chapter walks you through a fun, effective process for developing dynamite answers. And the next time you're asked one of these difficult questions, rather than cringe, you'll gladly rise to the challenge.

Risk It or Run From It?

- **Risk Rating:** In reality, nil, because right now you're just working on creating your answers. But it might make you sweat a little in private.

- **Payoff Potential:** Enormous. Being prepared for these questions in an interview might just help you seal the deal.

- **Time to Complete:** An hour or two.

(continued)

(continued)

- **Bailout Strategy:** Rely on the What, How, and Proof stories you developed in chapter 5 and polished in chapter 7. They might carry you through. But if you want to be better skilled at handling the traditional toughies and the unexpected curve balls an interviewer might throw your way, work on answers to these questions, too.

- **The "20 Percent Extra" Edge:** Planning and practicing tough-question responses allows Career Champs to reap better results than average interview candidates.

- **"Go For It!" Bonus Activity:** Rehearse your tough-question responses until you can pretty much say them in your sleep.

How to Tell an Employer About Yourself and Your Strengths and Weaknesses

If answering the "tell me about yourself" and "strengths and weaknesses" questions feels like an overwhelming task to you, the following exercises will help you develop effective, truthful responses using simple, step-by-step processes.

Develop Your "Tell Me About Yourself" Response

It seems as if an answer to this question should be easy (after all, who knows you better than yourself?). But for most Career Cowards, "Tell me about yourself" is the biggest fear-inducing query. Why? Because in just a few seconds, you have the power to make yourself look like Mr. Incredible...or Mr. Idiot.

Panic Point! Does the pressure make your knees knock? Never fear! Your great "tell me about yourself" plan is right here. Create a plan for what you're going to say, practice it until you feel comfortable, and you'll be in great shape.

Consider the following bits of personal and professional information (a little mix of both is best) to decide what you want to share about yourself:

- Where you're from originally and how you came to live in your current location

- A few of your hobbies or interests

- What type of work you're aiming for

- A brief listing of former positions and employers

- What people say are your strengths

- A real-life example (maybe one of your What, How, and Proof stories) that demonstrates one of your strengths

- A brief overview of your educational credentials

- Something interesting or unusual about you

- A statement about why the job is especially appealing to you

To begin developing your "tell me about yourself" answer, find some index cards or sticky notes. Use a separate card for each of the preceding items and jot down a sentence or two about each topic. For instance, on "a brief overview of your educational credentials," you might write this:

> "After high school, I pursued an associate degree to help me learn more about accounting. A few years later, I went back to school for my bachelor's in accounting, and last year earned my CPA."

For the "something interesting or unusual about you," try something like this:

> "A few years ago, I biked from coast to coast across the United States with my father."

Once you've written your responses, spend some time experimenting with the pieces you might want to include and their order. Rearrange the pieces and practice your response over and over until you find a set of elements in the order that feels good to you.

As with your What, How, and Proof statements, you'll want your "tell me about yourself" response to be just a few minutes long, to avoid losing the listener's interest. When you've got an answer that feels good to you, practice, practice, practice until you can practically tell-you-about-yourself in your sleep! That way, when you're sweating and nervous in the interview, you'll have a no-brainer reply to get things started successfully.

Develop Your Strengths and Weaknesses Response

Other frequently asked interview questions are "Give me a list of your strengths and weaknesses," "What's your biggest weakness?" and "What's your greatest strength?" Again, your replies to these questions have the potential to make you look like a champ or a chump. You (of all people!) should know your assets and liabilities. To build a great response, let's take this question one piece at a time.

Brainstorm Your Strengths

To create your reply to the "strengths" part of this question, jot down a few thoughts about each of these items on a separate index card or sticky note:

- What is one skill or characteristic that you are complimented on frequently?

- What are you often asked to do because you're so good at it?

- What skill or activity comes easily to you because you seem to have a natural talent for it?

- What quality about yourself are you most proud of?

- If you asked your mother to list one of your strengths, what would she say?

- What have you received high marks for on performance reviews or on school assignments?

As an example, here are my answers:

- Complimented frequently on ability to get things done.

- Often asked to write things.

- Writing comes easily to me.

- Most proud of my ability to focus on the highest priorities.

- My mother would say I'm creative.

- I received high marks for my ability to create a plan and implement it.

Again, spend some time playing with your responses to these questions, choosing two or three to use as content for the "strengths" part of your answer. Depending on what you choose, you might want to include a What, How, and Proof story to serve as evidence of that strength. For instance, a "strengths" reply that also includes a What, How, and Proof story to support my strength in writing would be this:

> "One of my strengths is writing. As an example, I did some research about my local newspaper and discovered that readers had interest in having a career advice column once each week. I put together some sample columns, sold the idea to the editor, and have been writing a column every week for the past 11 years—that's over 500 columns! The column has become one of the most popular in the paper. It's the only one that runs every week, and it's been placed on the front page of the business section. Plus, I regularly receive compliments from readers on how much they like my advice and writing style."

Panic Point! You might be you saying to yourself, "Do I really have any strengths about myself to describe?" or "Won't I sound like a bragger if I talk about my strengths?" Yes, braggers are boring. But not being able to articulate your strengths doesn't make you appear modest—it makes you sound weak or incompetent. This plan allows you to create something truthful (not "braggy") and present it in a factual, comfortable way.

One helpful approach is to lead your strength statements with "Other people have complimented me on my ability to…" so that you don't have to feel as though you're blowing your own horn.

Another consideration: Ideally, if you're interviewing for a job that's a good match for your talents and interests, your strengths will closely align with the requirements for the job. For instance, if you're interviewing for a sales job, and one of your strengths is being able to build great long-term relationships, it would be in your best interest to share that information about yourself because those two pieces fit together so nicely.

Finally, remember the basic parameters regarding your strengths answer: Keep it to just a few minutes, and practice it enough times that you feel comfortable having it come out of your mouth.

Brainstorm Your Weaknesses

Develop your weakness response by following these guidelines:

- Choose a weakness that you sincerely consider to be a flaw, but that you've taken steps to improve.

- Choose a weakness that isn't a "deal breaker" for the job. For instance, if the position requires you to provide customer service, don't describe one of your weaknesses to be "I get impatient with people."

- Choose a weakness that you have the potential to improve, rather than a character flaw that is unlikely to be changed. "I sometimes have a messy desk when I get busy" is due to a lack of skill in organization, and can be corrected by learning better systems for keeping things in order. "I have a bad temper" is a character flaw that typically isn't easily corrected.

Brainstorm five weaknesses to see which one or two might be used in an interview. As an example, here's my weakness list:

1. I have a hard time delegating because I want to control the outcome of everything I'm involved in.

2. When I get too busy, I drop the ball on some details.

3. There are times when I don't speak up about things that bother me.

4. Sometimes I want to rescue the people I love from the pain they're going through, and as a result stick my nose in where it doesn't belong.

5. I am sometimes lazy about picking up my clothes at the end of the day.

Now let's consider the potential of each:

1. **"...hard time delegating..."**: This one is a possibility because delegation can be learned, and I've actually been delegating more lately with some good results, so I'd have something positive to say about my growth in this area.

2. **"...drop the ball on some details..."**: I don't think I'd use this one because an employer probably wouldn't want to hire someone who admits to dropping the ball on details. Could be a deal killer.

3. **"...don't speak up about things that bother me."**: This one has potential, again, because I've gained some better skills in this area recently. For instance, I've learned that if something someone does is still bugging me after 48 hours, I should probably have a mature conversation with them about how I feel.

4. **"...rescuing people I love..."**: I think I'd skip this one. Sounds too personal, plus it might fall into the category of character flaws.

5. **"...lazy about picking up clothes..."**: I could use this one if I wanted. It's not a character flaw, and it's something I could easily work on improving. But overall, it seems kind of trivial and not related to work, so I'll skip it.

That leaves me with weaknesses 1 and 3—enough statements to work with for developing an interview response. I'll want to include these two elements in my final answer:

Weakness Point #1: A to-the-point description of the weakness, without going into gory detail. On the "...hard time delegating..." weakness, I could say,

> "In the past, I've had a hard time delegating because I wanted to make sure that the outcome of something turned out a certain way."

I wouldn't, however, want to elaborate too much by also saying,

> "In fact, one time I took on a big project and didn't share tasks with my team members. In the end, we missed the project deadline by more than two months, and my employer lost that customer's future business, worth over $2 million to the company each year."

Yikes! Too much information!

Weakness Point #2: A statement about how you've strengthened this weakness or are in the process of improving it.

> "About six months ago, I attended a workshop on how to delegate effectively, and I learned some new strategies I was willing to try. Since then I've been delegating more, with good results. It's been a little uncomfortable for me, but I can definitely tell that I'm improving in this area."

Aim to develop at least two or three weakness statements (each just a minute or two in length) and practice these until you can deliver a to-the-point description of each fault, along with your past or current improvement strategy.

Why It's Worth Doing

"Tell me about yourself" is one of the highest-stake questions you can be asked in an interview. As a question that typically shows up early in the conversation, your answer provides you the opportunity to bomb, or soar, right from the start. Preparing and practicing your "tell me about yourself" response is one of the best groundwork steps you can take to help you make a great impression while significantly reducing your interviewing anxiety. Like money in the bank, a solid "tell me about yourself" response gives you confidence and security.

The same is true for having a powerful reply to "Describe your strengths and weaknesses." Again, this is one of the most popular interview questions of all time, so you can pretty much count on having to come up with an answer to this one. So why not put in the time to create and rehearse a winner? It's well worth the effort.

Career Champ Profile: Josie

Josie was working on her tough-question responses. "Tell me about yourself," I prompted her. She squirmed in her seat. "Uhm, I worked for the local community college for 12 years. I had a lot of jobs there. Now I want to find a job that I enjoy better." I know Josie is a talented, likeable person, but if I was hearing about her for the first time in an interview, I wouldn't be impressed.

"What do people say that you do well?" I asked her. "I'm really organized," she began excitedly. "And I'm great at remembering details about things. I'm like a walking encyclopedia. At the college, people figured out that if they wanted to know what had happened there at one time or another, they could ask me and I'd probably know."

"Where're you from originally?" I continued. "Iowa. But my family moved to Colorado when I was in high school so my dad could take over his father's car business."

"What do you like to do for fun?" I continued. "I garden, and I volunteer a lot for a nonprofit organization that helps children improve their reading skills."

"What kind of job would you love to have?" I asked her. She answered, "Something in purchasing. My attention to detail and organization work well for finding and tracking the best prices on supplies. I handled the purchasing function in my last job at the college. I was good at it. My boss said I was better than anyone he'd known in the last 15 years at keeping adequate supplies on hand and staying within the purchasing budget."

"Let's put these pieces together as a 'Tell me about yourself' reply," I suggested. Then I laid out some notes in front of her to read through:

> "I'm from Iowa originally, and I moved to Colorado when I was in high school. I love to garden, plus I spend time volunteering at a local nonprofit organization that helps children improve their reading skills. Professionally, I'm aiming for a position in purchasing. That was my most recent job at the community college, and my boss said I was great at it. I was able to stay within budget and keep needed supplies on hand better than anyone else he'd worked with in the last several years. People compliment me on my organization and on my ability to remember details. In fact, at my job at the college they started calling me 'The walking encyclopedia' because I could remember all kinds of things that had happened there in the last 10 years."

"Wow!" I raved, "That sounded great! We just need a final transition statement and you'll be in great shape." Josie added, "And the reason I'm so excited to interview for your position today is that...."

Core Courage Concept

Coming up with effective answers to "tell me about yourself" and "describe your strengths and weaknesses" is scary—but not having a solid response in an interview is even more frightening. Pushing through your fear of "What will I say?" and developing answers that allow you to promote yourself successfully boosts your confidence and will significantly improve your interview results.

Confidence Checklist

☐ Develop your "tell me about yourself" response.

☐ Develop your "strengths and weaknesses" response.

Chapter 9

Get Ready for a Traditional Interview

You're probably familiar with how a traditional interview operates: You arrive, the interviewer asks you predictable things like "Tell me about you," or "Where do you want to be in ten years?" and you spout out answers. But have you ever *really* taken the time to analyze and practice your responses to these popular questions?

And have you ever looked closely at what you're saying in response to sensitive topics, such as, "Have you ever been fired?" Take time now to carefully examine the most popular questions, along with your responses. Most likely, this review will uncover several opportunities for you to improve your interview results.

Risk It or Run From It?

- **Risk Rating:** Once again, no real risk at this point—just thinking, writing, and practicing.

- **Payoff Potential:** If you like the feeling of being well prepared, the gain is definitely worth the work.

(continued)

(continued)

- **Time to Complete:** Quick-and-dirty version—30 minutes. More complete prep—a few hours.

- **Bailout Strategy:** Skip this chapter and you could still probably do alright by relying on the What, How, and Proof stories you developed in chapters 5 and 7. But why not spend a few minutes looking at the question lists anyway—just for fun—to see how you do?

- **The "20 Percent Extra" Edge:** Although it's impossible to prepare for every question you might be asked, preparing for several definitely gives you an edge.

- **"Go For It!" Bonus Activity:** Write up and practice a response to every interview question included in this section.

How to Get Ready for a Traditional Interview

Statistically, you're more likely to encounter a traditional interview format than any other kind of interview, so it makes sense to learn how they operate, as well as how you can respond best to certain questions. Here you'll gain an inside perspective on traditional interviews, review a list of the most popular questions, and learn valuable guidelines for answering them.

Learn About Traditional Interviews

Traditional interviews are, by far, the most common interview format. These interviews are most often comprised of widely known and predictable questions, such as "Tell me about yourself," "Describe your strengths and weaknesses," and "Where do you want to be in five years?"

Although traditional interviews are not nearly as effective as techniques such as behavioral or situational interviewing (which you'll learn about in the next chapter), they continue to be the most popular style of interviewing. Why? Because hiring managers have passed down the practice from one worker generation to the next. Also, most companies don't have human resources departments to make the hiring process any better. Three quarters of today's organizations employ relatively few workers (less then 25), and in organizations of this size, a formal HR department is thought unnecessary.

As a result, interviewing at a small business is usually pretty seat-of-the-pants, as in, "Oh! I'm interviewing you today! Let's see…what shall I ask you…?" By the time a candidate walks in the door, many hiring managers haven't prepared a single interview question. Instead, they hope they'll be able to come up with something to talk about based on your resume. The results are usually poor. Ever been in an interview where the interviewer spent most of the time talking about himself? Relying on his ability to think on his feet, the interviewer fails to come up with effective interview questions and instead ends up talking about the topic he knows best: himself.

But even if the interview you encounter is a disorganized traditional format (and even if the interviewer can only think of things to say about himself), you can make a traditional interview process work for you with these techniques:

- Ask the interviewer, "What do you see as being the most important experience a person should have to succeed in this position?" Listen carefully to her answer. After she's finished, say, "Oh! That reminds me of some experience I've had with that topic." Then respond with one or two What, How, and Proof stories highlighting your background in those areas.

- Use your knowledge of the company to guide the conversation. "Ms. Interviewer, I read an article that talked about your company's recent launch of a new product. In my last position, I was part of a very successful new product launch plan within the customer service department…" followed by a relevant What, How, and Proof story.

- Have on hand a list of questions for the interviewer (I discuss this in greater detail in chapter 12), and ask questions such as "What projects do you need done, and in what order?" Choose questions that will provide you a great lead-in to related What, How, and Proof stories about your strengths.

Prepare Responses for Traditional Interview Questions You May Be Asked

Review this list of popular traditional interview questions, asking yourself how you'd respond to each:

1. Tell me about yourself.

2. Why should I hire you?

3. What are your major strengths?

4. What are your major weaknesses?

5. How does your previous experience relate to this job?

6. What are your plans for the future?

7. What will your former employers say about you?

8. Why are you looking for this sort of position and why here?

9. What are your future plans?

10. How do you spend your spare time? What are your hobbies?

11. What jobs have you held? How were they obtained?

12. What courses did you like best? Least? Why?

13. Why did you choose your particular field of work?

14. What do you know about our company?

15. What qualifications do you have that make you feel that you will be successful in your field?

16. What are your salary requirements?

17. If you were starting school all over again, what would you do differently?

18. Why did you decide to go to the school you attended?

19. How did you rank in your graduating class in high school? Other schools?

20. Do you think that your extracurricular activities were worth the time you devoted to them? Why?

21. What do you think determines a person's progress in a good company?

22. What personal characteristics are necessary for success in your chosen field?

23. Why do you think you would like this particular type of job?

24. What kind of boss do you prefer?

25. Can you take instructions without feeling upset?

26. Tell me a story.

27. How did previous employers treat you?

28. What have you learned from some of the jobs you have held?

29. What interests you about our product or service?

30. When did you choose a major?

31. Have you ever had any difficulty getting along with fellow students and faculty? Fellow workers?

32. Which of your school years was most difficult?

33. Are you willing to go where the company sends you?

34. What job in our company would you choose if you were entirely free to do so?

35. What types of books have you read?

36. What types of people seem to rub you the wrong way?

37. What jobs have you enjoyed the most? The least? Why?

38. What are the disadvantages of your chosen field?

39. Do you think that grades should be considered by employers? Why or why not?

40. What are your major accomplishments?

41. Give me an example of a time when you saved money for your company.

Question list adapted from Michael Farr's Next-Day Job Interview *(JIST Publishing).*

The secret to responding successfully to traditional interview questions is taking the time to think through your answers *before* the interview. As with any question you might be asked, developing a successful answer saves you from blurting out something you'll later regret. For instance, when asked, "How do you manage stress or conflict?" in an interview, you wouldn't want to answer "I kick back with a cold brew or two" (even if it's true!). The interviewer doesn't want to think he's hiring an alcoholic.

Look through the list and decide how you want to answer each question. If you get stuck on any question, review your What, How, and Proof stories for inspiration. Often, there are great responses buried in your best success stories. Follow these Interview Answer Rules when deciding what you want to say.

Rule #1: Never, Ever, *Ever* Blame or Badmouth a Former Employer

No matter what offense has been committed against you, avoid saying anything that sounds like, "My former boss/company did this bad thing to me." Even if you were seriously mistreated, any negative statement you make about a former employer sticks to you like a bad smell. The interviewer will view you as having an attitude problem, instead of viewing your former employer as having an employee-treatment problem.

The interviewer will also be thinking, "Gee, I wonder what bad things he'll be saying about me six months from now…." Better to avoid the topic altogether. If you do find yourself being pressed to share negative details, opt for a reply such as, "There are certain details about that situation that I believe are better not to discuss. I hope you'll respect my privacy on that topic."

Rule #2: Be Judged Based on What You Share

Certain religious and political affiliations can brand you positively or negatively in the eyes of the interviewer. For instance, you might be an active member of the National Rifle Association and enjoy hunting. A large percentage of interviewers will be offended by your hobby, so it might be better to choose a different pastime to describe. However, if it's important to you to work with like-minded coworkers, sharing details about your beliefs early in an interview will allow you to sniff out a mismatch before you're ever offered the job. If you're not comfortable being evaluated on your political or religious beliefs, don't share them at all.

Rule #3: Never Pass on the Blame

Take full responsibility for any frustrations you might have experienced in your career. Avoid blaming any person or situation for blocks or disappointments you might have experienced. Similar to badmouthing a former employer, blaming someone or something other than yourself for a disappointment comes across as childish. For instance, rather than, "My parents wouldn't let me study music in college, so I had to choose a career path I didn't enjoy," take responsibility for your part in the situation. "I chose to support my parents' wishes and pursue a practical degree in college. However, I have a great love of music and have hopes of obtaining additional training in that field in the future."

It might take you a while to identify the part you played in a frustrating circumstance, but it is there. Even if all you can say is "I would have hoped things would have gone differently, but they didn't. So I picked up from there and moved forward." Owning your part in disappointments allows you to present yourself as adult and responsible—two very attractive qualities in potential employees.

Rule #4: Be Specific with Positives and General with Negatives

When responding to a question with a positive slant, answer in specifics, such as, "My favorite boss was Karen. She gave me plenty of opportunity to share and experiment with my ideas." When replying to questions that have a negative slant, such as "What kind of people do you find it most difficult to work with?" keep things vague. For example, "The few times I've had difficulty dealing with people were times when people didn't follow through on a commitment."

Why It's Worth Doing

Preparing responses to interview questions is like squirreling away money in the bank: You never know when you're going to need them, but it's a huge relief just knowing they're there.

Career Champ Profile: Geri

Geri had been fired from her last job and the "Have you ever been terminated?" question terrified her. "They'll think I'm such a loser!" she worried. When we started working on her response to this question, it was obvious she had a lot of frustrations built up about her former employer.

Motivated to help Geri come up with an effective response, I reminded her of interview answer rules #1 (never badmouth a former employer), #3 (never pass the blame for a disappointment), and #4 (keep responses to negatively slanted questions general). Geri's short "I worked for them for more than 10 years. Then they fired me, just like that. They were so unfair," swiftly violated all three of them.

"Let's begin by reworking the employer-badmouthing part," I said. "What can you truthfully say about your employer or the industry that may have impacted what was going on at that time?" Geri thought for a moment. "Well, a new manager had just joined the company. And on top of that, there were new regulations being imposed on the industry. It made everything pretty confusing for a while."

We were starting to uncover some useful information. I wanted more: "And what was your part in what happened next?" A pained expression passed over Geri's face; she sighed heavily. "I'd been doing things the same way for a long time. When we got the new manager *and* all the regulation changes, I guess I felt pretty overwhelmed. In some ways I froze up. They wanted me to try new things, and I probably wasn't always as flexible as I could have been."

The picture was becoming clearer: Big changes happen in the company. Established employee freaks and digs in heels. But now we needed a good ending.

"What did you learn from that situation?" Geri's face lit up and she laughed. "What started out as being a bad thing turned out to be a really good experience for me overall. I needed a change, but I hadn't realized it. As soon as I left that company, I went back to school to take more computer classes. The skills I learned opened my eyes to so many new career interests and opportunities, and I'm really excited about that. I don't want to get myself stuck in a rut like that again."

We worked on putting together the key pieces of Geri's response to "Have you ever been terminated?"

> "Yes. In my last position, there were big changes that happened within the company and the industry—new boss, new regulations. Not necessarily bad things, but different. I got a little overwhelmed at all that was going on, and I didn't make changes as fast as I probably should have. In the end, it turned out to be a positive experience overall, because I pushed myself out of my comfort zone to learn new things. Lately I've taken more computer classes and I love it. I never want to get myself stuck in that kind of rut again."

Core Courage Concept

It takes daring to look at yourself—the good parts as well as the bad. Yet thinking through what you want to say about yourself *before* you're on the spot in an interview gives you a much better chance of responding successfully. Sure, it takes a little time and effort—but it will probably land you in a job you want faster.

Confidence Checklist

☐ Learn about traditional interviews.

☐ Prepare responses for traditional interview questions you might be asked.

Chapter 10

Be Prepared for Not-So-Traditional Interviews

> **" "** And now, Ms. Candidate, we'd like you to tell us about a time when you persuaded some team members to do things your way. After that, we'd like you to show us how you'd prioritize items in a sample 'in-box.' And when you're through with those two things, we're taking you to lunch."

Sound like an unusual interview? Depending on a company's hiring process, you may encounter a wide range of interviewing challenges, from simple phone screenings to behavioral, situational, technical, and off-site interview formats. This chapter helps you successfully prepare for and respond to them all.

Risk It or Run From It?

- **Risk Rating:** Slim to none. Just more "on your own" activities, reading, practicing, and building your confidence muscles.

- **Payoff Potential:** Very high. Behavioral, situational, technical, phone, and off-site interviews stump a greater percentage of candidates than does traditional interviewing.

(continued)

(continued)

Mastering some strategies for each could set you apart in a very good way.

- **Time to Complete:** About the time it would take you to watch a mindless reality show or two.

- **Bailout Strategy:** See if you can fly with only your database of What, How, and Proof stories to keep you aloft (but spend a few seconds peeking at the questions to see how you'd do anyway).

- **The "20 Percent Extra" Edge:** Planning and practicing great answers to these popular behavioral questions will have you walking into the interview feeling as if you've got Confidence Insurance in your pockets. That in itself is a 20 percent advantage.

- **"Go For It!" Bonus Activity:** Create a document with your answers to all these questions, and then verbally run through each of them multiple times for practice.

How to Prepare for Not-So-Traditional Interviews

As an interview format used by more and more companies, you're likely to come across a behavioral interview or two along the way. The next few sections provide you with a basic understanding of behavioral interviews and then equip you to respond successfully to a wide range of behavior-based questions.

Learn About Behavioral Interviewing

"Behavioral" might sound a bit intimidating, like some complicated scientific or psychological process. To make it seem a little less scary, focus on the core of the word, "behave," and you've cracked the code for what behavioral interviewing is all about.

Behavioral interviews are designed to help an interviewer predict your future actions based on how you've *behaved* in the past. Research on interviewing shows that when a candidate is selected based on his or her answers to behavioral questions (as compared to answers to traditional questions), the organization stands a much better chance of making a good choice. As a result, companies with more advanced hiring processes tend to rely primarily on behavioral interviewing questions.

Most behavioral questions ask you to describe a specific instance or example from your past, often beginning with, "Tell me about a time when you…," and followed by something like

- …demonstrated your expertise in (a particular skill area).

- …adapted to a difficult situation.

- …delegated a project effectively.

- …surmounted a major obstacle, and so on.

Many people (especially Career Cowards) view these questions as being particularly tough, especially because they require you to come up with a specific, detailed response. Vague and general answers just won't cut it!

"Arrrgggggghhhhhhh!!" you might be thinking. "What if I'm asked one of these big, hairy behavioral questions and I can't think of an answer?" Stop. Take a deep breath, and visualize yourself in a tub of warm, cozy What, How, and Proof stories.

Yes! What, How, and Proof stories!! Remember those?! All that hard work you did in chapter 5 to develop some great stories will help you with answers to behavioral questions. And because you've already developed several of them (right??), you're way ahead of the game!

Say, for instance, you're asked, "Tell me about a time when you surmounted a major obstacle." Look back on your What, How, & Proof stories list and ask yourself, "Did I surmount major obstacles with any of these?" My guess is that you probably did. Bingo! That one's solved, now on to the next!

Learn What All the "Negative" Stuff Is About

If you peek ahead to the list of behavioral questions included in this chapter, you'll see that many of them are written with a negative slant, such as, "Tell me about a time when you were unable to complete a project on time."

Panic Point! You might be wondering, "Why do so many questions focus on negative experiences? Is the interviewer trying to make me look bad?" No, the interviewer is *not* trying to make you look bad. Rather, he or she wants to see how you react under pressure and whether you're able to learn from your mistakes.

None of us is perfect. But some of us are better at responding well to pressure and growing from our shortcomings than are others — and ideally, those are the individuals a hiring manager wants to add to his or her team.

By asking negatively slanted behavioral questions, an interviewer can examine a candidate's behavior in stressful situations. In many companies, a question like "Describe a conflict situation with a coworker" has become almost as popular as "Describe your strengths and weaknesses." And a candidate's answers to these questions can be as high-stakes as a response to "tell me about yourself." Consider this real-life example of what happened when a candidate, Dawn, was asked to describe a conflict situation with a coworker:

> "When I started my last job, I could see that a lot of things needed to be changed in the department where I was working. I started making those changes right away. The other woman who worked in that department got mad at me, but I knew my ideas were better than hers, so I held my ground. We never really got along. About a month later, she quit."

After Dawn's interview, the hiring team met to discuss their impressions. "She seems pushy," one manager said. "And insensitive," another added. Very quickly, the group decided that Dawn was not the kind of worker they wanted to add to their team, primarily because of her answer to the conflict question.

As you can see, answers to behavioral questions can be tricky. Unless you think them all the way through *before* you start telling the story, you might find yourself face-to-face with a story ending that doesn't make you look very good.

Here are some guidelines for choosing an effective What, How, and Proof story to use in response to a negatively slanted behavioral interview question:

- Choose a story that shows you took responsibility and grew from the situation. Although you might have made mistakes during the particular event, be able to describe what improved behavior you ultimately learned and implemented.

- Avoid stories that describe other people negatively. "My coworker's desk was always a mess" sounds judgmental. "My coworker had a different style of organizing his desk" sounds mature and tolerant. Instead of describing another person's behavior as "bad" or "good," present it as "different."

- Share facts, rather than feelings. Facts allow you to present a story honestly and clearly, without imposing unfair opinions. For instance, "My last boss was a micromanager" is your own assessment about your last manager's behavior. "My last boss wanted me to show him every customer order I prepared" is a specific fact about how your boss behaved.

- Whenever possible, wrap up the What, How, and Proof story you use for a negatively slanted question with "And what I learned from that experience is…."

Try a Run-Through

Now it's time to read through the following list of popular behavioral interview questions and ask yourself how you'd answer each. Some, like the question "tell me about a time when you had to fire a friend," might not apply to you, so skip over those. For the rest, use your database of What, How, and Proof stories and see what answers might work for you.

Tell me about a time when you…

1. Demonstrated your expertise with _____. (Fill in the blank based on one of the key requirements of the job.)

2. Worked effectively under pressure.

3. Handled a difficult situation with a coworker.

4. Were creative in solving a problem.

5. Missed an obvious solution to a problem.

6. Were unable to complete a project on time.

7. Persuaded team members to do things your way.

8. Wrote a report that was well received.

9. Anticipated potential problems and developed preventative measures.

10. Had to make an important decision with limited facts.

11. Were forced to make an unpopular decision.

12. Had to adapt to a difficult situation.

13. Were tolerant of an opinion that was different from yours.

14. Were disappointed in your behavior.

15. Used your political savvy to push a program through that you really believed in.

16. Had to deal with an irate customer.

17. Delegated a project effectively.

18. Surmounted a major obstacle.

19. Set your sights too high (or too low).

20. Prioritized the elements of a complicated project.

21. Got bogged down in the details of a project.

22. Lost (or won) an important contract.

23. Made a bad decision.

24. Had to fire a friend.

25. Hired (or fired) the wrong person.

How did you do? If you're like most people, you've come up with answers to only a few of them this first round. Tackle a few at a time, giving yourself a period in between to allow your brain to mull over possible replies. As you come up with effective answers, add them to your list of responses. Eventually you'll have them all handled.

Learn About Phone, Situational, Technical, and Off-Site Interviews

Although they are less popular than traditional and behavioral interview formats, you may occasionally encounter phone, situational, technical, or off-site interview setups. Following is a brief description, along with some helpful tips, for each.

Phone Interviews

More and more often, candidates are screened through a phone interview before they're scheduled for a face-to-face meeting. Typically conducted by a recruiter or human resources representative, the primary purpose of a phone screening is to review your background to determine whether you possess the basic qualifications needed for the position. If you pass the phone screening, you'll be scheduled for a face-to-face interview. Following are some tips:

- Prepare as you would for an in-person interview, including analyzing the position's key skills; developing What, How, and Proof stories that highlight your background in those areas; and practicing your responses to popular interview questions.

- Have your resume and lists of your accomplishments handy to use as a reference during the interview. One advantage to a phone screening is that you can use cheat sheets!

- Stand up, rather than sit down, throughout the interview. It will add energy to your voice.

- Smile as you talk, just as you would in an in-person conversation. It changes the tone of your voice in a positive way.

Situational Interviews

Situational interviews can come in many forms, all of which—in one way or another—put you in the position of having to respond to a particular *situation*. For instance, it might be a hands-on examination of your expertise, such as a typing test or an assignment to sort through and prioritize an actual company in-box. Or it might be a verbal "what-if" examination: "What would you do if X happened?"

Technical Interviews

Technical interviews surface when there's some practical knowledge required for the job, such as how to engineer a widget or calculate a result. To succeed in this type of interview, most technical managers recommend that you refresh yourself on the basics before the interview. For instance, if it's an engineering or accounting position, review the foundation skills you learned for your profession.

Whatever type of interview challenge you encounter, take a deep breath and make sure you understand what's being asked of you *before* you respond. If you're not clear on the question or assignment, ask for clarification. The interviewer will be more impressed that you took the time to comprehend the task in advance, instead of deciding to jump in unprepared—and failing.

Off-Site Interviews

You might be invited out for lunch, dinner, drinks, or a plant tour. Although these might feel more informal than an in-the-office, nose-to-nose meeting, be careful not to get too relaxed. If you're offered an alcoholic drink, and if the other members of your group are having one, too, order something light and have only a few sips.

When it comes to food, choose items that are easy to eat without making a mess. Bottom line, never forget that you're still being closely scrutinized, even if it feels as though you're being treated as one of the gang.

Why It's Worth Doing

As with Dawn, a misstep with a behavioral question could quickly land you in the "do not hire" pile on a decision maker's desk. Taking the time to think through effective responses in advance can save you from hanging yourself in the interview. The short-term pain of brainstorming and planning your responses to these questions is well worth the long-term gain of presenting yourself more successfully in an interview.

Career Champ Profile: Steven

"Describe yourself in one word," I grilled Steven during his interview practice. "Dedicated," he answered. "How would your last boss describe you?" I continued. "Plays well with others. Great communicator." "Now, tell me about a time when you had a conflict with a coworker." Steven had been working on this one. His first few attempts portrayed him as being stubborn and mouthy. In our last meeting, I'd given him some suggestions, and I was anxious to see how his new and improved conflict answer had come together.

"Well, at my last job, I was responsible for the packaging for a new software product. Looking at the competition's packaging, I knew we needed a spiffier-looking box. But it cost more than the previous packaging. The manufacturing manager was doing his best to drive down costs. He didn't like that my new packaging was going to cost more. We ended up getting into a heated argument on the manufacturing floor one day.

"I knew this wasn't the way to resolve the problem, so I asked him if we could take a 30-minute break and then meet again in his office. He agreed. In those 30 minutes, I pulled together some important cost numbers to show him.

"Back in his office, I made the point of telling him that I appreciated all the work he'd done to lower costs, and showed him a report that proved manufacturing costs had dropped by 20 percent in the last year. Then I told him that I, too, was interested in reducing expenses where it made sense. To back up that point, I showed more information that proved I'd reduced marketing costs by 15 percent over the last year while increasing sales by 25 percent. 'We're working toward the same goals.' I reminded him.

"Then I wrapped things up by saying that while I wanted to keep costs down, I was also motivated to keep sales growing, and that I felt that better packaging was an important step toward making that happen. I kept my cool and relied on the data to tell the story. In the end, he agreed to support my packaging plan, and we had more respect for each other in the future.

"What I learned from that experience was that sometimes it makes sense to take a break when there's a conflict going on. I also learned that data is helpful in making a point. It keeps things objective. I've used that 'take a break' and 'rely on data' strategy several times since in conflict situations. It works great!"

Core Courage Concept

We all have ups and downs in our lives…and we respond better in some situations than in others. Having the courage to sift through our many experiences to find and practice the best examples of our own behavior *before* an interview gives us a better chance of presenting our best self to others when it really counts.

Confidence Checklist

☐ Learn about behavioral interviewing.

☐ Learn what all the "negative" questions are about.

☐ Try a run-through.

☐ Learn about other types of interviews.

Chapter 11

Build Your Confidence Inside and Out

Chances are you're already feeling much better about your ability to perform well in interviews. And you should! All the hard work you've put into developing and practicing What, How, and Proof stories and understanding different interview techniques has already significantly improved your interview skills.

Now you'll put even more polish on your performance, with the following practical and highly effective techniques for everything from delivering a confident handshake to keeping your cool when an interview gets stressful.

Risk It or Run From It?

- **Risk Rating:** Still pretty low. The toughest part (if it seems tough to you) will be interacting with some image helpers.

- **Payoff Potential:** Big. With these steps, you can pull together all the hard work you've done so far and create a fabulous self-presentation.

- **Time to Complete:** A few minutes to a few hours, depending on how much time you choose to invest.

(continued)

(continued)

- **Bailout Strategy:** If you're feeling rock-solid confident about how you present yourself, inside and out, skip it.

- **The "20 Percent Extra" Edge:** Ever seen someone enter a room who looks extra-specially fantastic and conducts himself or herself with confidence? That could be you.

- **"Go For It!" Bonus Activity:** Pull together your inside and outside presentation pieces, and then stage a practice debut with someone who believes in you.

How to Build Your Confidence

Maintaining confidence is an inside *and* outside challenge. You want your outside appearance to project self-assurance; plus, you want to feel it on the inside, too!

The following techniques provide step-by-step guidance for attaining, and maintaining, a cool, confident you. Begin by analyzing and improving your inner self through tips on self-talk, eye contact, your smile, handshake, listening skills, and managing interview stress. Then move on to enhancing your outer persona—including hair, face, and dress—to achieve the ultimate positive impression.

Test Your Inside Confidence

Rate the following statements about yourself, using a 1–10 scale (with 1 being "never," 10 being "always," and 2–9 being somewhere in between):

- When I meet someone new, I am able to greet them with a confident smile, a firm handshake, and steady eye contact.

- When I'm talking with someone, I am able to concentrate successfully on what they're saying to me.

- When faced with a situation that makes me uncomfortable, I am able to manage my emotions and continue to think clearly, even though I may not know exactly what to do.

How'd you do? If you scored low on most or all of these, you're reading the right book! (If you scored 8 or above on all of them, skip to the next section.) The actions in the preceding list can be difficult for even the most confident people. Yet many who are able to do these things well have discovered that even though they might not feel rock-solid-confident on the inside, they can fake self-belief and poise until it becomes second nature.

Build Your Self-Confidence

These confidence-building techniques will bring you closer to projecting impressive self confidence.

A Confident Smile

For a smile that's just right, smile hard, and then relax it just a little. The corners of your mouth should be turned up slightly, but not too much. Practice it over and over until your mouth settles in that position almost automatically.

A Firm Handshake

Like a good joke, having a good handshake at your disposal comes in handy. As you reach for the other person's hand, the web between your thumb and pointer finger should touch the other person's web. (Avoid the "end-of-finger grab" style of handshake. Too girly, even for girls!) Your fingers should then curve gently around the outside of the other person's hand (no stiff-as-a-board or curly cupped fingers) before you squeeze gently. Grip as if you were checking for their pulse under their skin. Steer clear of manly-man crushes or half-hearted wimpy squeezes. Hold for a slow count of three before releasing. To remember the key steps, think "web-curve-squeeze." If your palms tend to sweat, coat your skin with a little antiperspirant before the interview.

Steady (but Not Searing) Eye Contact

Because "eyes are the windows to a person's soul," the eye-contact thing can be a toughie for most of us. A balance between looking into a person's eyes long enough to come across as interested and confident, but not so long that the other person feels stared at, is a good goal. If looking directly in the other person's eyes is too uncomfortable, look at the space between his or her eyes instead. And it's fine to break eye contact for brief periods.

Maintaining Concentration under Stress

This boils down to listening—being able to process and comprehend what you're hearing—without getting distracted by your own concerns. When someone else is talking, most of us (Career Cowards especially) are usually thinking about what we're going to say in response. But because our brains can't successfully handle two conscious trains of thought at once, neither line of thinking gets handled effectively.

For those of us who plan our response before the other person has finished, we usually do so because we're afraid we won't be able to think of something to say. "Better get working on this now!" we think. But as we've already determined, if you're thinking about your reply, you're not listening to all of what's being said. This is a dangerous situation, especially in an interview.

To improve your listening and concentration skills, focus on what's being said by leaning toward the speaker and consciously processing what you hear. When your brain attempts to butt in with its own thoughts, tell it, "Your turn is coming. I promise."

If it helps, ask permission to take notes as the other person is speaking. This can work especially well in an interview. Taking notes allows you to write down phrases that help you focus on key concepts. In addition, the person who's talking feels as if you're making his or her comments a high priority. And, while you're writing down notes about what the speaker is saying, you can also jot down key phrases about thoughts that pop into your brain, and then refer to those notes later to assist you in your reply.

Managing Your Emotions Effectively, Even When You Feel Uncomfortable

No doubt about it, interviews are nerve-wracking! We want to present ourselves successfully while trying to get through one of the most stressful events known to man. Of course we're going to get emotional!

Panic Point! When our emotions get in the way, it's usually because, subconsciously, we want to protect ourselves from harm. If we feel nervous or panicked, it's often because we're afraid that we're going to be hurt somehow. In the case of an interview, that typically means being rejected. For some people, that feeling of panic results in talking a lot, saying anything that comes to mind in hopes that something will work out okay. For others, it means shutting down and saying very little: "If I keep my mouth shut, maybe I won't screw up." In an interview, neither talking too much nor saying too little is a good way to go. Better to learn some management strategies to use when panic sets in.

These three self-talk techniques will help you stay calm and composed:

- **"I'm prepared."** And you will be! By identifying the key requirements for the job; developing What, How, and Proof stories that showcase your expertise in those areas; and practicing your responses to the most popular interview questions, you will be much better prepared than most of the other candidates. Rest calmer knowing you're in good shape, because you *are*.

- **"I like myself."** I learned this one from motivational speaker Brian Tracy, and it has been one of my personal favorite confidence boosters ever since. At any time you feel nervous about how you're doing, tell yourself (silently, of course), "I like myself, I like myself." It sends a strong, fast message to your brain that you're okay.

- **"I'll do well."** Your preparation, combined with the effective techniques described in this book, *will* help you do well in the interview.

So in an interview, when panic begins to push into your consciousness, repeat these statements to yourself. Your emotions should come right back in line.

Evaluate and Boost Your Outside Confidence

Rate the following statements about yourself, using a 1–10 scale (with 1 being "never," 10 being "always," and 2–9 being somewhere in between):

- I'm comfortable with the appearance of my hair.

- I'm comfortable with the appearance of my face.

- I'm comfortable with the appearance of my body.

- I have at least two interview outfits that I know I look good in and feel great wearing.

Again, if you scored high, move on to the next section. If you scored 7 or below on any of these statements, keep reading.

Get Comfortable with the Appearance of Your Hair

The best piece of advice I ever got about a great hairstyle is to be on the lookout (walking down the street, in the mall, wherever) for someone with hair similar to yours who has a great haircut, and ask them who did it. Then, even if it's pricey, have that stylist cut your hair once each year, relying on a less-costly stylist to keep it in shape for the trims in-between.

As with most appearance-related decisions, stick with tasteful, classic styles unless you're interviewing for a position requiring someone with extreme artistic creativity.

Get Comfortable with the Appearance of Your Face

As the part of your body that gets the most attention, it's worth investing time and effort in worthwhile improvements. Teeth whitening can give you a big confidence boost for a reasonable cost.

For women, a makeup consultation with a specialist at a department store (seek out someone whose makeup you like—and lean toward lighter rather than heavier application) can help you decide what to wear and how to apply it effectively. If you can't afford the price tag of the department-store cosmetics, take note of what you need and find something comparable at a discount store.

For men, neatly trimmed facial-hair is essential. If you're interviewing for a job in a professional office environment, it's best to avoid beards and mustaches altogether, especially for job interviews. After you're hired, you can evaluate the acceptability of growing and wearing facial hair.

Get Comfortable with the Appearance of Your Body

Although you won't be able to achieve a total body makeover in time for an interview scheduled for next week, you can significantly improve your body confidence by choosing clothes that flatter your shape. And if you don't already exercise regularly, at least begin walking. The endorphins released during exercise will make you feel better about yourself almost immediately.

Find Two Great Interview Outfits

Do you have two interview outfits that you know look great on you—clothes that when you wear them, help you feel good about yourself and prompt others to comment on how nice you look? If not, this might be an excuse to go shopping!

Begin by determining the level of attire that is appropriate for the interview. You want to dress one level *above* what you would normally wear on the job every day. If you're not sure, either call the receptionist and ask him or her about the organization's dress code, or hang out in the company's parking lot at the start or end of the business day to scope out the norm. The goal is make a good impression and look as though you fit in, too.

For instance, if the environment is…

- **Business dressy:** Wear a matched suit (coat and slacks/skirt) in a neutral color (but not black). Ties for men. Stockings for women.

- **Business casual:** Opt for a jacket and complementary slacks/skirt. Again, ties and hose are required, and stick with neutrals.

- **Casual or work uniform:** Choose a collared shirt and complementary slacks/skirt.

Lean toward conservative styles, especially for interviews. You can show your more unique flair *after* you land the job.

You'll want two complete outfits so that you can alternate them for first, second, and subsequent interviews. If you're at all unsure of what to choose, head for an upscale clothing store and track down a tastefully dressed sales associate. Ask him or her for suggestions on what will flatter you and meet the dress-code criteria. Again, if the items are too costly for your budget, make notes on the specialist's suggestions and then hunt down less-expensive alternatives elsewhere. Secondhand stores can be an excellent source for interview attire. Complete your spiffy new look with quality shoes in good condition.

Again, enlist the help of a supporter (a friend or advisor you trust) to give you a final okay on your appearance.

Why It's Worth Doing

All the work you've been doing to this point—identifying a position's key skill areas; creating and practicing your What, How, and Proof stories; and developing answers to popular interview questions—have been like individual pieces of confidence you've been collecting. Techniques to build your self-belief inside and out will allow you to cement those pieces together to create a total confidence package.

Career Champ Profile: Jenn

When Jenn got laid off, she'd been working at the same bank for almost 20 years. Because of this, she hadn't worked on her inside or outside interview appearance for almost two decades, and she desperately wanted a boost.

I sent her on a field trip to a local department store to work on her wardrobe. When she showed up the following week wearing one of her new outfits—a great-fitting deep burgundy jacket, matching skirt, crisp white blouse, and complementary scarf—it was obvious that she was already feeling better about herself. "What do you think?" she said, smiling broadly. "After the clerk at Macy's told me what to look for, I headed over to that nice secondhand shop in Old Town and found this suit. It only cost me $30! I had the sleeves on the jacket and the hem on the skirt altered so that it fit me better."

I could tell that Jenn's outside appearance was boosting her inner confidence as well. As she told me the story of her shopping expedition, she smiled easily and looked directly at me. "Nice work!" I complimented her, and reached out to shake her hand. Her grasp was warm and strong.

Core Courage Concept

Trying new confidence-boosting strategies can feel awkward. "Are they really necessary?" you might wonder. Yet techniques that improve your appearance on the outside, combined with fake-it-'till-you-make-it internal confidence boosters, can go a long way toward launching you into a higher level of interview performance.

Confidence Checklist

☐ Test your inside confidence.

☐ Reinforce your inside confidence.

☐ Evaluate and boost your outside confidence.

Part 2

Face and Overcome Your Interviewing Fears

Chapter 12

Get the Interview Off on the Right Foot

People handle basic introduction steps automatically, from a smile and handshake to the first "hello." Yet small improvements in how you execute them can make a huge difference in how you come across. Improve the impact you make with your first impression through these image-enhancing techniques.

Risk It or Run From It?

- **Risk Rating:** A little steeper now—you'll be making contact with the interviewers. But it will be okay. You're well prepared to have things go successfully.

- **Payoff Potential:** High. "First impressions" and all that.

- **Time to Complete:** About an hour for the pre-interview work. Just a few minutes for the actual start of the interview.

- **Bailout Strategy:** You can skip the pre-work (although it will calm your nerves and further build your confidence) and jump right into the introduction.

- **The "20 Percent Extra" Edge:** Having a plan for a successful interview launch will portray you as a candidate who's got his (or her) act together!

(continued)

(continued)

> • **"Go For It!" Bonus Activity:** Practice the intro steps—the greeting, handshake, and starter small talk with a friend a few times, to work out the kinks and make it seem more familiar.

How to Get the Interview Off on the Right Foot

The pieces of your confident interview are starting to come together: You've identified the key skill areas for the job; developed and practiced some killer What, How, and Proof stories; and learned some stellar strategies for projecting confidence inside and out. Now it's show time: The interview is about to begin, and all your hard work will pay off. Just a few more details to handle…

Decide What to Bring

Consider this list of possibilities:

> ☐ Several hardcopies of your resume on quality paper.
>
> ☐ Multiple copies of any other documents you might want to have on hand, such as a listing of your references and an "Accomplishments" page that includes highlights of your best What, How, and Proof stories.
>
> ☐ A copy of the job description.
>
> ☐ Directions to the interview and a phone number for the site.
>
> ☐ A portfolio, including three to ten examples of your best work, such as a sample of a well-received report, a drawing for a product you engineered, or a photograph of a bookcase you installed. Whatever you choose, be sure that it's highly relevant to the position for which you're interviewing.
>
> ☐ A small notepad, to record names of people you meet, details of questions you're asked, or other important information.
>
> ☐ Business cards or calling cards.

□ Extras of anything you're worried you might want more than one of (such as stockings, antiperspirant, a white shirt, and so on).

□ Your favorite "pump me up" music to play on the drive to the interview.

□ Your cell phone (in case, due to an unforeseen emergency, you're running late—but be sure to turn it off before you go into the interview).

□ Warm and fuzzy confidence builders, such as a photo of your family or a "You can do it!" audio recording from your significant other.

Although your resume is the only "must have" on this list, being able to easily lay your hands on some of the other items might go a long way toward helping you feel more prepared and confident.

Panic Point! An Accomplishments page is a great confidence builder/cheat sheet to use in case you draw a blank sometime in the interview. You can always pull it out if you're in a panic and say, "I've brought a listing of my accomplishments..." and scan it as you decide how you want to answer their question.

Scope Out the Location Early, but Arrive on Time

My office in Fort Collins, Colorado, is located on one of the city's main streets. When I give people directions to my building, many times they will say, "Oh! I know exactly where you are!" Yet when it's time for them to be at my office, many don't arrive on schedule. When that happens, I can usually expect a phone call about 10 or 15 minutes later, with the individual saying, "I can't find your office...."

When this happens, I can make some good guesses about that person: One, they're probably not very skilled in listening (they *assumed* they knew where they were going when I gave them directions, but they really didn't), and two, they didn't take the time to drive to my location in advance to be sure of the route.

If at all possible, drive to the site for the interview at least one day in advance, so that you know exactly where you're going. It will lower your stress level an additional few notches. And on the day of the interview, be exactly on time for your meeting, or no more than five minutes early. Arriving earlier than five minutes may create extra work for the receptionist or the interviewer, as they might need to make special accommodations for you.

If it turns out you'll be more than five minutes late to the interview, phone and let the interviewer know that you're delayed, and why. (And it had better be a *very* good reason!)

Master Your "Meet and Greet"

You've already mastered the Confident Smile; aced the web, curve, and squeeze handshake; and improved your eye contact by looking at the space between an individual's eyes. Now you'll put those pieces together for a successful meet and greet at the start of your interview.

As you wait in the reception area for your interviewer to arrive, use the time to review your resume and Accomplishments list. Silently remind yourself, "I'm prepared. I like myself. I will succeed." When you're approached by your interviewer, make eye contact, turn on your confident smile, and stand up. When the interviewer has almost reached the place where you're standing, take one step forward— but no more. This is important because technically, the interviewer is "in charge." By waiting for him or her to come to you, you show the interviewer respect.

When he or she arrives, extend your hand for a web, curve and squeeze handshake, and then give yourself a mental pat on the back. You're doing great so far!

Sail Through the Starter Small Talk

When it comes to small talk, "Hello, Mr./Ms. (fill in their last name). Thank you for the opportunity to meet with you today," is the best place to start. Then take a deep breath, smile, maintain eye contact, and pause for a few seconds. Chances are the interviewer will have a small-talk question for you, so listen carefully and respond appropriately.

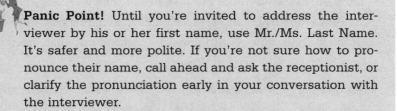

Panic Point! Until you're invited to address the interviewer by his or her first name, use Mr./Ms. Last Name. It's safer and more polite. If you're not sure how to pronounce their name, call ahead and ask the receptionist, or clarify the pronunciation early in your conversation with the interviewer.

As your small-talk conversation progresses, be alert for a lull in the conversation. That will be your opportunity to fill in with one or two small-talk questions of your own. One of my favorite small-talk memory tools is to recall the acronym, F.O.R.D., which stands for Family, Occupation, Recreation, and Dreams. Here are some possible small-talk questions based on the F.O.R.D. outline:

- Are you from this area originally?

- How long have you worked here?

- Has the company always been in this location?

- What do you like to do for fun?

- Any exciting adventures or trips coming up for you?

And remember, if you researched anything about the individual prior to the interview, you can work in some of those comments as well. For instance, "I see that you spoke at the Widget Builders Association last month. How did that go?"

A few other tips about small talk:

- Avoid controversial topics, such as politics and religion.

- Ask only one question at a time. It's common for Career Cowards (especially when they're nervous) to fire off several questions in quick succession, making it difficult for the interviewer to answer any of them effectively. Instead, ask one question at a time and really listen to the response.

- If it makes sense, follow your first small-talk question with another that builds on it. For instance, if she's just told you that no, she's not from this area originally, that she was born in another state, you could follow up with, "And what brought you here?"

- Realize that a little silence is okay. Allowing some quiet to seep into the conversation conveys that you are confident enough to keep your mouth shut sometimes.

Congratulations! You've successfully made it through the introduction and small-talk segment of the interview.

Why It's Worth Doing

Knowing where to stand and what to say in the first few minutes of an interview—a time when stress can be especially high—will greatly reduce your anxiety level. And if you can cut out a little more anxiety, why not go for it?

Career Champ Profile: Marnie

Marnie had an especially wimpy handshake. Like many women, she believed that lightly grasping another person's hand by the end of the fingers was more ladylike than a full-on handclasp. But rather than feminine, the effect was "fishy." Together we worked through several web, curve, and squeeze practice handshakes until Marnie's grip began to feel welcoming, rather than like a weak turnoff.

"Now, let's see some eye contact and your confident smile," I encouraged her. Like she was trying to pat her head and rub her belly simultaneously, Marnie struggled with putting the pieces together at first. "Just keep practicing," I prompted her.

After a few more tries, Marnie's web, curve, and squeeze, confident smile, and eye contact started to look and feel more natural. "It's a pleasure to meet you, Ms. Piotrowski," Marnie said to me as she added the first of her small talk into the mix. "Are you from this area originally?"

We were both a little awed at Marnie's exciting progress. "You're very impressive!" I told her. And she was. The leap in self-belief, from where Marnie had begun with a flimsy handshake, to her new-found skill in launching an interview like a poised professional—was as obvious as her confident smile.

Core Courage Concept

The first few minutes of an interview are typically the most nerve wracking. You've got new people to meet and great first impressions to make! By becoming skilled at the basics of a great greeting—your smile, eye contact, handshake, and small talk—you can reduce your stress and start feeling confident from the start!

Confidence Checklist

- Decide what to bring.
- Scope out the location early, but arrive on time.
- Master your "meet and greet."
- Sail through your starter small talk.

Chapter 13

Give Your Best Interview Performance

The more you know about what to expect in an interview situation, the more confident you'll be. Learning about a variety of interview formats, and having a toolbox of techniques for responding to stress-inducing questions, will significantly increase your ability to perform well.

Risk It or Run From It?

- **Risk Rating:** Pretty high—but you can take it. Remember, think "I'm prepared. I like myself. I'll do well!"

- **Payoff Potential:** Humongous! The rubber meets the road right here.

- **Time to Complete:** As long as it takes for you to get through the interview.

- **Bailout Strategy:** I guess you could call and cancel the interview. (But why do that? If for nothing else, use this opportunity to practice what you've learned so far.)

- **The "20 Percent Extra" Edge:** The preparation and practice you've already done will set you apart from the competition.

(continued)

(continued)

> • **"Go For It!" Bonus Activity:** Well...really go for it! Set
> aside your concerns about looking/saying/doing the right
> thing, and trust that your preparation and practice will carry
> you through, because it can!

How to Give Your Best Interview Performance

From a traditional one-on-one meeting to an engaging perform-this-task activity, interviewing comes in a variety of formats. Learn a little about each—along with effective techniques for dealing with stressful interview questions—and you'll boost your belief in your ability to present yourself well.

Understand the Interview Format

When you walk into an interview, you may find yourself in one of a variety of setups:

- A one-on-one interview with the hiring manager or an initial screening interview with a human resources representative

- A panel interview, made up of not only the hiring manager, but also team members and a human resources representative

- A group interview, involving the interviewer plus other candidates vying for the same position

- A presentation format, where you are asked to deliver a talk or complete a performance in front of an audience

- No one but yourself, tasked with completing some kind of task, such as a situational assignment or a personality assessment

Panic Point! Anything other than the traditional one-on-one arrangement might feel especially intimidating, especially to a Career Coward. But never forget your confidence chant, "I'm prepared. I like myself. I will do well."

Regardless of the format, if there are new people to meet, take the time to introduce yourself and learn their names. If there are several individuals, ask for business cards or for permission to take notes, so that you can jot down each person's name (and be sure you know how to spell it correctly). Then keep those business cards or your notes visible so that you can refer to each person accurately.

A few tips on conducting yourself with confidence in interviews involving multiple interviewers:

- When you're given a question, begin your reply by first making eye contact with the individual who asked it. As you continue talking, slide your eye contact slowly around to the other individuals in the room, until you've visually touched base with every person.

- Although the situation might feel stressful, don't forget the basics of your confident smile and eye contact. Your ability to connect successfully with people will be one of your strongest selling points.

Effectively Handle Questions

So you're really in the hot seat now, living through the test you've devoted hours to preparing for. These strategies will help you bravely and successfully handle the questions you're asked:

- **Buy your brain some time to produce a stellar answer:** Most Career Cowards panic a little whenever a question is presented. "Oh no!" you might think. "What if I can't answer this?" This is a perfectly normal response as your brain begins to get its act together. Often, all you need is a little extra time to allow the great answer to surface.

When you get that, "oh no!" feeling, buy yourself some thinking time by saying, "That's a really good question. May I have just a minute to think about it?" Not only does this give you a few extra seconds to ponder, it also gives the interviewer a little stroke, as he or she realizes, "Gee, I asked a *really good* question!"

- **Look at the question from a different angle:** At times, the question you've just been given will make no sense to you, either because your brain is in "oh no!" mode, or because it was worded strangely. If you don't understand what was asked, say, "Could you please rephrase that in a different way?"

- **Make "answer sandwiches":** An answer sandwich allows you to state, and restate, the question, inserting your answer in-between. This method allows you a stress-free start to your reply (you'll know *exactly* what to say), etches the question in your brain so that you stay on track with your answer, and communicates to the interviewer that you've successfully understood what's being asked of you. An answer sandwich is built like this:

    ○ First slice of bread: Rephrase and restate the question you've just been asked, such as, "So, Mr. Interviewer, you want to know about my experience in creating databases…."

    ○ Middle of the sandwich: Give your answer.

    ○ Second slice of bread: Again, rephrase the question you've been asked as part of your summary. "So that is some information about my experience creating databases."

- **Ask for a postponement:** If you're stumped on how to respond (but believe the answer is lurking in your brain somewhere), ask if you can come back to the question in a few minutes. Make a note of what you were asked so that you don't forget it. You can even say, "I'd like a minute to recall the details of an example I want to tell you about. Could we come back to this question in a few minutes?" Often, this has the effect of programming your brain to do its thing. And be sure you *do* come back to the question eventually. You don't want the interviewer to think you've wiggled out of a tough question.

- **Draw it out:** Answer not coming to you? Pull out your notepad and "draw it out." Write down a few key phrases. Or, if you can, diagram out the problem. As you do, verbalize your thought process for the interviewer. This can be an effective way to demonstrate how you solve problems while offering an interesting visual twist.

- **Give a parallel response:** If you don't have experience with the topic presented in the question, but you do have background in an area that's similar, provide a comparable answer. "While I don't have direct experience with what you're describing, I do have experience with something very similar...."

- **Use your cheaters:** Your resume, Accomplishments list, and portfolio can save you in an "oh no!" situation. When you know you've had experience with a particular topic but can't think of the instance immediately, say, "I believe there's a good example of my experience right here. Let me locate it for you...." Then look over your cheaters and see what comes to mind.

- **Manage inappropriate questions:** You might be asked a question that seems strange or inappropriate, such as "What is your religion?" or "Do you have any children?" This can be a sticky situation, because you don't want to come across as defensive or difficult. If the question seems blatantly improper, assume that you don't clearly understand what you're being asked, and request that the interviewer ask the question in a different way. If the question is still off color or rude, say, "I hope you won't mind, but I have a policy of not discussing personal matters unless they relate directly to the position. Does this job require that I practice a particular religion?"

Another question that could be considered inappropriate—depending on when it's asked—is the subject of salary and compensation. We'll review details about how to discuss and negotiate compensation in chapter 16. For now, keep in mind that ideally, the topic of money should not be discussed until you're made an offer. If you're asked, "What kind of money do you want to make?" respond with, "I'd feel more comfortable discussing that once we've determined that I'm the right person for the job. I hope you're okay with that." If you're pressed further to provide a number, bounce the question back to them with, "Since you know the company's pay scales, how about if you tell me what range you are thinking about, and I'll let you know if that sounds like it's in my ballpark?" If the interviewer holds the line on having you provide a compensation figure, offer a salary range that you've researched to be fair for the position.

- **Fess up (with a plan):** If you absolutely, positively don't know the answer to a question, admit it. But then describe how you would solve that problem in real life, as in, "Mr. Interviewer, I don't know the answer to that question. But the way I would find an answer would be…." Then talk about what you would do to find the information you'd need, such as contacting an expert or looking up information in a reference book.

Develop an Emergency Stress Plan

If you end up bombing on a question or two during the interview, it will be unfortunate, yes. But it's not the end of the world. If you do have a train wreck on an answer, keep it in perspective. If you want to start over, ask for permission: "I'd like a chance to answer this one again if I can…." The hiring manager isn't looking for the *perfect* candidate; he or she is looking for a qualified person who can manage themselves successfully in stressful situations, and this technique can help you demonstrate your own grace under pressure. Remember, too, that both you and the interviewer are human. Practically everyone can relate to being nervous in an interview. If you draw a blank, say something that sounds stupid, or do something that you're embarrassed about, own up to it. Say, "I'm really sorry. I'm just a little nervous. I hope you'll forgive me."

Why It's Worth Doing

One of the best ways to overcome your fear of something is to do it a few times. Preparing for and working through an actual interview—even if the thought of doing so terrifies you—helps you become more familiar with the process. Then, in your next interview, you'll be more accustomed to the process. Your fear will drop even more, and your performance will improve. Before you know it, you'll be doing great in interviews and feeling surprisingly comfortable!

Career Champ Profile: Bill

Bill had been extremely nervous about an upcoming interview for a senior researcher position at a small biotech company. He'd bombed in an interview a month before, and was worried about repeating his poor performance. To add to his stress level, this was a job that he *really* wanted.

To focus his nervous energy in a productive direction, Bill spent several hours in the days before the interview analyzing the position's key skill areas and developing several relevant What, How, and Proof stories. He also verbally practiced and refined his stories several times until he was happy with the result.

By the time the interview rolled around, Bill was feeling adequately prepared. He'd driven to the interview site in advance and selected a navy blue two-piece suit to wear the day of the interview. He took along a folder with copies of his resume and an Accomplishments list.

We met the day after the interview to debrief him on what had happened.

"They were more organized than I thought they'd be," Bill began. "They had five meetings lined up for me. First I met with a rep from human resources. She just wanted to walk me through my work history to understand the positions I'd held at each company. She also had me take one of those personality profile tests. It wasn't difficult, and I just answered honestly, because I wanted to come across as myself.

"After my talk with the HR rep, I met with the hiring manager, Corrine. She was great. I think she and I could really work well together. She asked me several of the questions that were on the traditional questions list. I drew a blank on one of them, 'Who are some of your heroes?' All I could think of was Mr. Incredible from that movie my son likes so much, and I didn't want to say that. So I asked if I could come back to the question a little later. She was okay with that. In a few minutes I remembered Lance Armstrong. I'm a biking fan, and I'd read in the hiring manager's company profile that she's a biker, too, so that turned out to be a good one to mention.

"After the hiring manager interview, I met with the team I'd be working with. They took me to lunch and interviewed me over the meal. A few of the team members ordered a beer, but I stuck with a Coke to be safe. And I ordered a chicken breast sandwich — something fairly healthy and easy to eat.

"Overall, the team was great. I think I could work well with them. My guess is that they'd been trained in behavioral interviewing techniques. They asked me several 'Tell me about a time…' kinds of questions. I had some good stories to share, and was glad I'd taken along my portfolio to show them some actual work samples. One guy did ask me sort of a weird question. 'Am I a Republican?' I came back with, 'I don't normally discuss politics or religion unless I'm forced to.' The group thought that was funny and laughed.

"After lunch I was expected to give a 30-minute presentation on my research specialty to the team, the hiring manager, and two managers from different departments. I'd known about the presentation — the HR rep told me that in advance — so I was ready for it. I did draw a blank midway through my presentation, and that freaked me out. But I told myself, 'I'm prepared. I like myself. I will do well.' Then I said, 'I just need a minute here...' as I reviewed my notes. I was able to pick up where I lost my place and the rest of the presentation went fine.

"It was a long day, but I did great! I was *so glad* that I put in the time to develop my What, How, and Proof stories, and to practice answers to questions before the interview. All day long, as people asked me questions, it was as if I had an interview expert in my brain helping me along, telling me to say this or show them that.

"And since I'd actually practiced my answers in advance, I felt much more comfortable. I discovered that I was able to focus better on their questions, knowing that I'd probably have a good response for whatever they might ask me. It made me more relaxed all the way around. I never thought I'd hear myself saying this, but the interview was actually fun!"

Core Courage Concept

Preparing for and performing well in an interview is a huge accomplishment. Yes, interviews are intimidating. Yes, there will be many times during the evaluation that you'll be shaking in your shoes. But knowing you've done your best to invest in yourself builds courage and success, and your interview results will be on an upswing from here.

Confidence Checklist

- ☐ Understand the interview format.
- ☐ Effectively handle questions.
- ☐ Develop an emergency stress plan.

Chapter 14

Wrap It Up Like a Champ

There you are, cooking along in the main part of the interview, answering questions and sharing What, How, and Proof stories like a pro. Over and over you tell yourself, "I am prepared. I like myself. I will do well." When you run into questions that stump or confuse you, you say, "Would you please rephrase that?" or "That's a great question. I need a minute to think about it." Then your brain kicks in at just the right time with a glorious answer. You're acing this interview.

After a while, though, it's obvious that the interview is winding down. The hiring manager starts to pack up his notes, and glances at his watch. He's wrapping up the interview. Another "oh no!" moment blasts through your brain, as you wonder, "Have I covered all my bases? What have I missed?" Now you'll learn just what to do to when you reach the home stretch of the interview.

Risk It or Run From It?

- **Risk Rating:** Critical (as in "Make it or break it" time). But rest assured, you'll be ready to handle it successfully.

- **Payoff Potential:** Major.

(continued)

(continued)

- **Time to Complete:** The time it takes for you to tie things up and make your exit.

- **Bailout Strategy:** Punt and skip over the recommended wrap-things-up-well steps. You'll end the stress of the interview sooner, but at what cost?

- **The "20 Percent Extra" Edge:** Most candidates are clueless about how to wrap up an interview effectively. By having a solid plan, you'll nail the finish and stand out from among the competition.

- **"Go For It!" Bonus Activity:** Create a discreet checklist of wrap-up "to do's" and refer to it before you say your final goodbye.

How to End the Interview Successfully

Coming into the home stretch in an interview can be such a relief. You're almost done! Yet don't miss out on these opportunities to finish strong and improve your likelihood of landing an offer.

Make Sure You've Covered All of the Important Bases

You've already analyzed the key skill areas for the position as part of your interview preparation. Now, as the interview begins to wind down, ask yourself, "Did I adequately describe my expertise, sharing at least one or two great What, How, and Proof stories for each key skill area?"

If the answer is "yes," pat yourself on your back. You're probably in pretty good shape in the self-promotion department. If the answer is "no," don't panic. There's still time. Somewhere in the next few minutes, you'll want to tell a show-stopping What, How, and Proof story that will leave the interviewer wondering, "How could I possibly live without this person on my team?"

This story-telling opportunity might present itself when you're asked, "So, why should we hire you?" (See the following section for more details on this question.) Or you might need to shoehorn the story in on your own. For instance, you might say,

> "Mr. Interviewer, I just thought of an example from my background that is particularly relevant to the skills needed for this position. May I share it?"

Another technique is to pull out your portfolio as you request the opportunity to share another example. If you haven't used your portfolio much (or at all) so far, this might be an excellent time to add some visual interest to the conversation.

Caution: If you find that you need to squeeze in another great What, How, and Proof story, keep it short. The interviewer might be on a tight time schedule, and you don't want him to feel as though you've cornered him in an endless blab session about yourself.

In addition to verifying that you've addressed all the key skill areas, confirm that you've answered all the questions you've been asked. You might have requested a postponement on a question that stumped you. This is the time to wrap up any loose ends on unanswered questions. If you're still drawing a blank on how to respond to a tough question, at least say,

> "Mr. Interviewer, I had hoped to have an answer to this question by now, but I don't. I would like to get back to you with a response by tomorrow. Would you prefer that I phone you or send it via e-mail?"

Know How to Answer "Why Should We Hire You?"

On par with "tell me about yourself," "why should we hire you?" is one of those high-stakes questions that can strike fear in the hearts of Career Cowards everywhere.

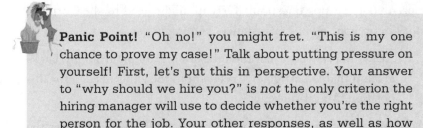

Panic Point! "Oh no!" you might fret. "This is my one chance to prove my case!" Talk about putting pressure on yourself! First, let's put this in perspective. Your answer to "why should we hire you?" is *not* the only criterion the hiring manager will use to decide whether you're the right person for the job. Your other responses, as well as how you've handled yourself up to this point, also count.

The reply you give to this question can be short and sweet, or more in-depth, depending on what you hope to accomplish:

- If you still need to address a key skill area or two, answer "why should we hire you" with something like this:

  "Well, Mr. Interviewer, I'd be the right person for the job because I have proven experience succeeding with responsibilities just like those required for this position. For instance, one time I..." (and then share a strong What, How, and Proof story).

- If you've done an adequate job of promoting yourself throughout the interview, you can provide a summary of what you've shared so far, as in the following:

  "Mr. Interviewer, as you've stated, you're looking for someone with strengths in the key skill areas of A, B, and C. Through the examples I've shared, particularly my experiences with [make reference to a few What, How, and Proof stories], I've demonstrated my ability to succeed in the most important aspects of this job."

- If you feel as though you've already done an excellent job of selling yourself and don't need to beat the interviewer over the head with it anymore, look him or her in the eye and say

  "Mr. Interviewer, I know I can do a great job for you, and I'd love the opportunity to prove it."

Have Your "Questions for the Interviewer" Ready

"Now, what questions do you have for me?" is a common let's-wrap-this-interview-up technique used by interviewers. Often, candidates are unprepared and will say something goofy like, "What would the job pay?" or "I think you've answered them all for me already!"

Both of these are poor replies. You should avoid any discussion of pay or benefits until you've been offered a job. Focusing on these topics too early sends an "all this candidate cares about is the pay and health insurance" message to the interviewer—not the impression you want to make! Plus, if you wait, you'll have more leverage to negotiate a competitive compensation package *after* the interviewer has decided he can't possibly live without you.

If you're concerned about the position's compensation, investigate typical pay ranges before the interview by checking with your network of colleagues to see what they know. You can also research average pay ranges through a salary Web site or through your professional association's annual wage survey.

Benefits questions are also taboo, as in, "Do you offer dental coverage?" or "I was planning on going to Mexico for two weeks next month. Would that be okay?" You'll have a chance to go over all these details *after* you've received an offer and *before* you accept it.

Now on to goofy reply number two: "I think you've answered them all for me!" This answer tells the interviewer that you didn't take the time to plan some questions in advance. Avoid this predicament by choosing three to five questions from the list below and writing them in the notepad you'll take with you to the interview. Then, when the interviewer asks, "Do you have any questions for me?" you can say, "Yes, I've written some down...."

- What do you see as this position's greatest challenge at the present?

- Why is this position open at this time?

- What are your immediate objectives and priorities for this position?

- What characteristics do you value most in an employee?

- Where does this position fit within your organization?

- What projects do you need done, and in what order?

- Please describe the culture of the company (for example, dress, energy level, and so on).

- How is performance measured, and how is successful performance rewarded?

- Please tell me about the training I would receive.

- How does this organization support professional growth?

- What does the company hope to accomplish in the next few years?

- If you could wave a magic wand and have the perfect person for this position, what would they be like?

- What could I do for you so that this time next year, your boss would think we're both geniuses?

Plan to fill about five minutes of time with your questions. Once you've reached that limit, wrap up things so that the hiring manager can move on with the interview.

State Your Interest in the Position
Saying

> "I would love to have this position and to be a part of your team"

is attractive to an interviewer. If you want the job, say so.

Walk Out the Door with Contact Information and a Next Step Clearly Defined
Frequently interviewers will end an interview by saying, "We'll let you know." This can put the candidate into a painful state of limbo: "He said he'd let me know. It's been six weeks. Do you think I'm still in the running? Agggggggghhhhhhh!!!!!!"

Save yourself from this purgatory by finding out more about the next step, as well as the hiring manager's anticipated schedule:

> "Mr. Interviewer, what will be your next step in this process? And when can I expect to hear something?"

These two details—the next step and the timeline—provide you valuable information helpful for following up after the interview. This is also a good time to exchange business or calling cards, so that you have ready access to the interviewer's contact information and the correct spelling of his or her name and can follow up appropriately (see chapter 15).

Why It's Worth Doing

Wrapping up an interview effectively is a "nice to do," but not a "*must* do." Yes, you can say, "I believe you've answered them all!" when an interviewer asks you if you have any questions. And you can bolt out the door as soon as the hiring manager says, "We'll be in touch," releasing you to escape to the comfort of your own home.

But before you take the easy way out, keep in mind what comes next: After you walk in your front door and kick off your shoes, you'll start wondering, "Did I highlight the best parts of my background?" and "What comes next?"

By taking the time to ensure that you've successfully covered your bases—double-checking that you've emphasized the most important aspects of your background, asking the interviewer a few questions, and determining the next step in the process—you not only end the interview well, you also set yourself up for next steps that will save you from an agonizing state of limbo.

Career Champ Profile: Pamela

Even though she'd been extremely nervous before, it was obvious that Pamela now felt great about how the interview for a financial consulting position was going. All her hard work preparing had paid off. Her eyes were sparkling and she was smiling confidently as she shared example after example of her relevant What, How, and Proof stories. She was even managing her "oh no!" reactions successfully, eventually responding in a good way to each question she was asked.

Then the hiring manager made the first move to wrap things up: "Why should we hire you?" she asked. Pamela ran a quick mental check of the position's key skill areas: financial knowledge, ability to advise and influence others, and computer skills. Had she addressed all of these areas adequately with her examples? Yes, she decided, she had, so she decided to provide the interviewer a summary, "sandwich" style:

"Why should you hire me? From what I've heard from you, Ms. Interviewer, you need someone in this position who has extensive knowledge of the financial products you represent, as well as knowledge about how to advise clients on wise financial investments. As I stated earlier, my successful experience providing financial information and support to clients at my job in North Carolina demonstrates my ability to succeed in this type of position.

"Additionally, my computer skills are strong, and my track record for bringing in new business has been excellent. You should hire me, Ms. Interviewer, because I have what it takes to do a great job for you!" Pamela's confident smile flashed again.

"Now, what questions do you have for me?" the interviewer asked.

Pamela reviewed the questions she'd written on her notepad and proceeded to ask the interviewer about her priorities for the person filling the job, as well as how Pamela could make them both look like geniuses by this time next year. The interviewer laughed at Pamela's second question before answering. "You could help me make this office the top-performing branch in the district, with the highest rate of new business and the most satisfied clients." "I'd love to!" Pamela replied, laughing along with her.

"Well, I guess we're done for now," the interviewer said, pushing back her chair to stand. Pamela stood, too, and asked, "So what happens next, and when?" The interviewer explained that there were two more days of first-round interviews and that they would begin second interviews the following Tuesday. "You should hear from me by Friday afternoon," the hiring manager said.

Pamela handed over a calling card with her contact information and received a business card from the interviewer. She then thanked the interviewer for her time, looked her in the eye, gave her a web-curve-squeeze handshake, and said, "I'd love to work with you." They said their goodbyes and Pamela headed to the parking lot.

Pamela was so excited about how she'd performed in the interview that on the way home she felt as if she were flying. "Whoa! Wow! I did great!" she thought to herself. Even though she wasn't sure what would happen next, she felt wonderful about how she'd prepared and performed so far. "Hooray for me!"

Core Courage Concept

Even though it might feel a little scary, taking the time to wrap up loose ends—like making sure you've communicated the most important parts of your background, asking the interviewer a few questions, and finding out what comes next—makes it easier for you to succeed with the next step in the interview process. And it's the small, step-by-step successes in the interviewing process that lead to the bigger ones down the line.

Confidence Checklist

☐ Make sure you've covered all of the important bases.

☐ Know how to answer "Why should we hire you?"

☐ Have your "questions for the interviewer" ready.

☐ State your interest in the position.

☐ Walk out the door with contact information and a next step clearly defined.

Chapter 15

Follow Up Effectively (and Fearlessly!)

You made it! You prepared, practiced, and performed your way brilliantly (or at least passably) through the interview. Good for you! Now, you wait for the results. But unlike the old-time dad pacing the hospital corridor waiting for his baby to be born, you don't need to be (and shouldn't be!) passive. There are many practical steps you can take to boost your chances of receiving an offer and improve your chances of success with other interviews in the future.

Risk It or Run From It?

- **Risk Rating:** In the middle—not too high, not too low. You can definitely handle it.

- **Payoff Potential:** Whopping. Effective follow-up can prompt a job offer.

- **Time to Complete:** A few minutes to an hour or so.

- **Bailout Strategy:** Don't follow up at all. Just cringe in the corner and pray for an offer. Maybe it will come.

(continued)

(continued)

- **The "20 Percent Extra" Edge:** The vast majority of job searchers don't follow up after an interview. Those who do follow up create more successes simply by pursuing opportunities in an organized way.

- **"Go For It!" Bonus Activity:** Create a step-by-step list of every interview follow-up activity and systematically complete every step for each interview.

How to Follow Up After an Interview

Job opportunities can be won or lost on your after-interview follow-up activities. Simple steps like sending a thank-you note, providing the interviewer promised information, and checking back on the status of the hiring process can land you in the premier-candidate slot...even if you weren't the #1 choice when you walked out the door. The following sections give tips on what to do after the interview is over.

Analyze Your Performance and Determine Any "Next-Round" Improvements

You made it through the interview. You're alive, kicking, and maybe even energized at how well you handled yourself. Or maybe you're frustrated that you didn't do better. However you're feeling, you can benefit from analyzing what you did well, and what you didn't do so well, in this interview. Conduct a thorough post-mortem of your interview:

1. Write down every question you can remember being asked in the interview, along with notes about your answers.

2. Determine which answers could use an overhaul, either by adding some more detail to a What, How, and Proof story or by coming up with a completely new response.

3. Analyze your nonverbal and confidence performance, including your appearance, eye contact, smile, handshake, and small talk. What, if anything, needs additional work?

4. Follow through on your action plan for improvement.

Finish Up Any After-Interview Action Items

Did you promise the interviewer you'd provide him or her with more information about your background or a response to a question? Make it a priority to wrap up any unfinished business as soon as possible.

Write and Send a Thank-You Note

When I lead workshops on interviewing, I routinely ask every person in the group to close their eyes (for confidentiality) and then raise their hand if they send a thank-you note after an interview. On average, only about 20 percent of people do.

The other 80 percent don't send thank-you notes because 1) they don't know what to write, and 2) they believe thank-you notes are unnecessary. Although thank-you notes aren't *required*, I do believe they're an important step in the interview process. The interviewer has agreed to spend time with you and has considered you for a position. Thanking him or her for this opportunity is a polite thing to do. And, taking into account that only one in five people prepares and mails a thank-you note, sending one makes you stand out in a good way.

What should you write? You can compose an effective job interview thank-you note in four easy steps:

Step 1: Thank the interviewer for his or her time.

Step 2: State—or restate—why you believe you're a good fit for the job.

Step 3: Make it clear that you want the job.

Step 4: Sign your name, and mail or deliver it.

Here's an example:

December 12, 20XX

Dear Mr. Smith,

      Thank you for interviewing me earlier today for the Customer Service Specialist position.

      After talking with you about the position requirements, I'm even more convinced that I'd be an asset to your organization. My experience in client services will allow me to come up to speed quickly.

      I look forward to hearing your decision regarding this position. The opportunity to work with you and the XYZ Company would be very exciting for me. Thank you again.

Sincerely,

Bob Brownard

Figure 15.1: A sample thank-you note.

That's it! You can add more if you want—such as a few sentences about how impressed you were with a certain aspect of the interviewer or the company. Here are a few guidelines for putting your note together:

- Make sure that you spell the interviewer's name correctly. Having the interviewer's business card is helpful for this purpose. If you don't have his or her card, check the company Web site or phone the receptionist and ask for the spelling information.

Panic Point! Don't assume that you know the spelling of a person's name. Consider these ways to spell John Smith: John Smythe, Jonne Smith, Jon Smythe. A person's name is the most precious phrase in their vocabulary. It's worth it to take the time to discover the correct spelling. One time I put together a proposal to provide career counseling services to a business. I was one of five consulting services bidding on the opportunity, and I called the company receptionist to confirm the spelling of the decision maker's name. I then listed it correctly on the cover sheet. The decision maker told me later that of the five bidders, only two had spelled her name correctly. She'd thrown out the other three proposals.

- If there is more than one interviewer, send a separate note to each person. If you interviewed with several people (more than five), send thank-you notes to the leaders of the group and request that they forward your appreciation on to the others.

- Choose a communication method that best suits the interviewer. For instance, if you're interviewing for a technical position, or with a technical company, and most of the communication happens electronically, send your thank-you note via e-mail. Otherwise, send a handwritten note (typed is fine if your handwriting is difficult to read). Use simple stationery—no duckies, flowers, or bunnies.

- Send your note within 48 (preferably 24) hours of the interview. If for some reason you take longer than that to get it in the mail, send it anyway. "Better late than never" applies when it comes to job interview thank-you notes.

Check Back at the Right Time

When you wrapped up your job interview, you learned about what would happen—and when—in the next step in the interview process: "We'll be calling on Friday," or "Second-round interviews begin next Tuesday. We'll let you know." So what happens if they said they'd get back to you but haven't? First of all, don't panic.

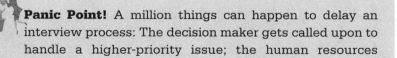

Panic Point! A million things can happen to delay an interview process: The decision maker gets called upon to handle a higher-priority issue; the human resources

(continued)

(continued)

department delays the next step as they research competitive compensation; the company CEO decides to stall new hiring until the end-of-the-month sales figures are posted. Although we wish the hiring process would be uninterrupted, it rarely is. More often than not, something holds it up.

Even though things might be delayed on the hiring company's end, you still want to stay informed. Knowing what's going on allows you to keep things moving forward in your own life. And no, you won't be bugging the hiring manager by checking back. In fact, decision makers (especially the effective ones) are impressed with candidates who follow through. So if you didn't hear anything by the time you were told you would, use the "three strikes, you're out" strategy for following up. Your first attempt should include a message like this:

"Hello, Mr. Interviewer. This is Julie Brown. When I interviewed with you last Thursday, you mentioned that a next step would be decided by Tuesday of this week. I wanted to check in with you about the status of the hiring process. I'm still very interested in the position. I can be reached at (953) 555-1212."

Notice that the message does not say, "You said you would call me by Tuesday and you didn't." At no point in your follow-up do you want to blame the interviewer for dropping the ball. State the facts ("…you mentioned that a next step would be decided by Tuesday…") without assigning any fault.

Your message can be delivered via e-mail, voice mail, or through a conversation on the phone. Choose whatever method feels most doable to you.

Panic Point! Does this follow-up step terrify you? If so, you're not alone. On average, even fewer people follow up after an interview than send thank-you notes! This is because people are worried they'll run into the big, ugly "R"—rejection. They fear they'll hear, "We don't want you."

Yes, there is the chance that you'll receive a rejection (more on that in chapter 17). There's also a chance that your follow-up will prompt a positive response (see the Career Champ Profile later in this chapter). So take the risk!

After you've left your first check-back message, wait 24 to 48 hours before following up again. When you do, use an alternative communication method. For instance, if you sent an e-mail with your first check-in, use voice mail for your next attempt.

Panic Point! If you worry that the hiring manager might actually answer the phone when you call, keep in mind that you can leave a voice mail outside of regular business hours, say, before 7 a.m. or after 7 p.m.

When you do make your second check-back attempt, use this type of script:

> "Hello, Mr. Interviewer. It's Julie Brown again. I left a message yesterday, and I wanted to make sure you'd received it. You mentioned that a next step in your hiring process would most likely be decided by this time. I'm still very excited about your opportunity, and I look forward to hearing from you about where we go from here. I can be contacted at (953) 555-1212, or through my e-mail at juliebrown@email.com. Thank you for your time."

Typically, a second check-in message from you will result in a response from the hiring manager. But if for some reason you *still* haven't heard back within two days of your second follow-up, it's time to deliver your third and final check-in. Send it via any communication method you prefer:

> "Hello, Mr. Interviewer. It's Julie Brown again. I'm guessing that you must be extremely busy or away from the office. Please know that I'm still very interested in the position and would love the chance to work with you and your organization. My phone number is (953) 555-1212, and I'll wait to hear from you. If for some reason I wasn't selected for the job, I wish you and the company great success with the person you did choose. As new opportunities become available in the future, please keep me in mind."

That's it! You've completed a thorough, "three strikes, you're out," follow-up process. Although you might not have received the response you hoped for, you can feel good knowing that you've followed through in a professional manner.

Don't Live in Limbo

Frequently, job searchers believe that having something to hope for (even if it's an empty hope) is better than having nothing at all. For this reason, they believe it's better to not follow up, especially if the news will be bad.

Although the head-in-the-sand approach is a strategy, it's not a very effective one. In fact, I've known people who have hung onto false hopes about receiving a job offer for up to six months after they interviewed. "Maybe they're still deciding," they say. Yikes! Talk about being stuck!

Getting the hard facts about whether you're the chosen candidate allows you to plan and act on the next step in your life. So be brave and follow up. Rarely is limbo better than reality.

Why It's Worth Doing

Less than 20 percent of candidates execute a thorough and effective follow-up effort after an interview. "It's not important," they believe. Or, "I'd rather not know if it's bad news."

Hiring methods are, by nature, loose processes. Consider what a hiring manager has to go through just to make a decision about bringing in a new employee: Do we need to hire someone? If so, what kind of background do we need? Who should we interview? Does this person meet our criteria? Should we make them an offer?

The hiring manager is faced with *so* many subjective factors when it comes to making a hiring decision. By conducting a thorough and organized follow-up process, you add a much-appreciated sense of order to the hiring manager's life. If he or she is waffling at all on who to hire, your effective follow-up process might help him or her in their decision.

Additionally, by executing a quality follow-through effort, you raise the hiring manager's perception of you even more. So even if this job isn't offered to you, the hiring manager will have an excellent impression of you for future opportunities.

Career Champ Profile: Paul

Paul had interviewed for a position as a director of a drug and alcohol awareness department at the local university. It was an exciting opportunity for him, and he was pleased with how he'd presented himself in the interview.

After the interview, Paul analyzed his performance (pretty good overall, he decided) and wrote and mailed a thank-you note to the three people he'd met with during the interview. Chloe, the hiring manager for the position, had told him they'd be getting back to him within 10 days.

Ten days had passed (12, in fact) and Paul was starting to worry. "Should I call?" he asked me. "What if they don't want me? I'd almost rather not know!" I told Paul I thought a follow-up call was a good idea, even if it did mean hearing a rejection.

Four days later, Paul phoned me. "I called," he began. "I was *really* scared when I dialed the number, but I kept my script for what I wanted to say right in front of me. Chloe answered the phone on the second ring. My voice was shaking, but I read my notes and got through it. And guess what?! Chloe told me that she'd been having a difficult time making a decision between me and one other person—that our two resumes had been sitting on her desk, staring her in the face. Since I'd called to check in, she decided to just offer the position to me, and would I be able to start on Monday? I got the job!"

Core Courage Concept

No doubt about it, it takes *guts* to follow up after an interview. More than 80 percent of people don't even risk it. Don't be one of those eight-in-ten people cowering in the corner! There are clear, doable action steps you can take that will keep the interview process (and your life) moving forward—steps that can actually *motivate* the hiring manager to make you an offer. Can you do it? Of course! Will it be scary? Probably. But you'll survive...and you'll feel better about yourself for doing it.

Confidence Checklist

☐ Analyze your performance and determine any "next-round" improvements.

☐ Finish up any after-interview action items.

☐ Write and send a thank-you note.

☐ Check back at the right time.

☐ Don't live in limbo.

Chapter 16

"I Got an Offer! Now What?"

Wow...all your hard work—the preparation, practice, performance, and follow-up—is paying off. You interviewed for a job, did fabulously well, and now the hiring manager has made you an offer! You're so excited; you just want to scream, "Yes! I'll take it!" But the logical part of you is saying, "Slow down there, buster. Is this what you really want? And if so, what do you need to negotiate to make it a win-win opportunity on both sides?"

Well, hang onto your excitement as you learn some excellent tips for evaluating and negotiating an excellent job offer.

Risk It or Run From It?

- **Risk Rating:** Lower than you might expect. You know they already want you. You're just hammering out the details.

- **Payoff Potential:** Sizeable. Coming to an attractive agreement will pay off for you in many ways down the line.

- **Time to Complete:** Could be a few minutes to a few hours over a period of a few days.

- **Bailout Strategy:** Grab the first offer and run with it. (But chances are you'd be disappointed with yourself later.)

(continued)

(continued)

- **The "20 Percent Extra" Edge:** Most people are too chicken to negotiate. Those who do gain more rewards, and more respect, from themselves and others.

- **"Go For It!" Bonus Activity:** Begin practicing your negotiation skills right away. Take some of what you learn in this chapter and attempt to negotiate a better deal with a service provider, in a store, or at a garage sale. The more you practice negotiation, the more comfortable—and successful—you'll become.

How to Evaluate and Negotiate a Great Job Offer

Money-talk can make even the most level-headed job searchers lose their senses. Yet a poorly negotiated salary can haunt you for years. To achieve the best compensation package possible, master the basics of successful salary negotiation *before* you find yourself in a high-pressure money discussion.

Learn When (and When Not) to Discuss Money

One key to successful negotiating is timing. For instance, when it comes to talking about money, the person who reveals specific details *first* is in a weakened negotiating position. For example, let's say that you've told the interviewer, "I need at least $40,000 to take this job," early in the interviewing process. The hiring manager then knows *exactly* what you think you're worth. He or she might perceive your figure as being too low ("Gee, I was thinking I'd have to pay at least $50,000 for someone good"), too high ("Yikes! There's no way I could afford this guy!"), or just right ("Hooray! He's right on the money!").

If at all possible, the topic of pay shouldn't be discussed until *after* the hiring manager decides you're the right person for the job. By then, you would have gained a thorough understanding of the requirements for the position, as well as insights into what the job is worth.

On the employer's side of the equation, he or she would have acquired enough knowledge about how you can benefit their organization to know your true value to them.

Unfortunately, though, discussions about money frequently pop up *before* an offer is made—sometimes even during the call to schedule your first interview: "So, Ms. Candidate, before we can schedule your interview, we need to know how much money you want to make."

Keeping in mind that 1) you don't want to tip your hand first, and 2) you'd rather wait until you've received a job offer, you'll want to reply with something like this:

> "Ms. Interviewer, I would feel more comfortable discussing pay after we've determined that I'm the right person for the job. I hope you're okay with that."

Usually this statement successfully puts off the money discussion for a while. But if you're pressed for further details, as in, "I need to know whether we can even afford you before I can continue the interview process," respond with:

> "Yes, that makes sense. It sounds as if you're working within a certain pay range. Since you're familiar with your company's pay scale, how about if you tell me the range you're thinking of, and I'll let you know whether it sounds fair to me."

If the interviewer provides a range that seems too low to you, don't squawk. It's very likely that you'll be able to negotiate more pay *after* they've interviewed you and decided that you're the best person for the job. For now, regardless of the range, simply say,

> "I think we should keep talking."

If the interviewer *still* presses you for details on what you want for pay, as in, "No, Ms. Candidate, I need to know what *you* want," provide pay information that you've researched from compensation sources such as www.salary.com, www.acinet.org, or your professional association's annual salary survey:

"That's fine, Ms. Interviewer. A salary for this type of position, as researched in a variety of up-to-date sources, shows that a pay range between $X and $Y is competitive."

Use the word "range" rather than a specific figure. This gives you more flexibility to negotiate down the line.

If at any point during the interview the hiring manager says, "Well, would you take the job for $X?" clarify whether you're actually being offered the position:

"Ms. Interviewer, are you offering me a job?"

If not, again request that you postpone any specific talk about money until after they've decided that you're the chosen candidate.

In summary, follow this order of discussion for money talk *before* an offer is made:

- First, postpone talk of money if possible.

- Second, request information about their range.

- Third, present your researched range.

Create Your Wish List

If you haven't done so already, think through what you really want in a job offer.

Compensation

What pay range is competitive for your type of work? What are you worth? Remember the important difference between *worth* and *need*. Your worth is a measure of the benefit you can offer to an employer. For instance, let's say that you've been involved in your career for five years. You're definitely not an entry-level worker who would need to settle for beginner's pay. However, you're not as skilled as someone with 10+ years of experience, either. Your worth will most likely fall somewhere in the middle of the pay range. Your value to an employer might also be calculated based on the price of the business you can bring to the organization, in terms of new sales or cost savings.

To determine your worth to an employer, research competitive pay ranges for your specialty and industry using information found on salary Web sites or through your professional organization. You can also approximate the value of your contributions to former employers by calculating how you've helped those organizations save and make money.

Now, on to the topic of *need*. Need is an estimate of what you would require to maintain your lifestyle. If your house payment is $1,000 a month; your car is $400; and food, clothes, insurance, and other extras run you $600; you *need* an income of $2,000 a month. However, when it comes to negotiating, your needs shouldn't enter into the discussion at all. Instead, you'll want to focus on your *worth*. It gives you far better negotiating power. "I need $2,000 per month to survive" sounds weak and desperate. "I know I'm worth between $40,000 and $50,000 to your organization" is perceived as attractive and assertive.

So calculate your worth to the organization and add it to your wish list, along with any other items you want:

- Competitive pay range
- Bonus for performance
- Vacation time
- Benefits (or extra compensation to cover the cost of benefits)
- Professional association memberships
- 401(k) or profit sharing
- Sponsorship to attend at least one industry conference each year
- Other

The Nature of the Position

In addition to the compensation portion of your package, think about the nature of the position. What tasks and responsibilities do you want? Any other considerations you need to discuss at offer time, such as how you prefer to work?

It's a good idea to actually write down your wishes. That way, when it comes time to negotiate your offer, you have a concrete list to which you can refer.

Negotiate the Initial Terms of the Offer

"We'd like to offer you the job." These seven words can kick off an exciting chain of events, offering potential for new opportunities, challenging responsibilities, and motivating rewards. But negotiating an offer is a highly charged emotional experience, so it's important to make use of sound negotiating strategies.

Begin by learning how to negotiate the best initial terms possible. For great tips, consider this sample negotiation between Shane, the candidate, and Bridgett, the hiring manager:

> **Bridgett:** "Shane, we'd like to offer you the job. How much money will it take to bring you on board?"
>
> **Shane:** "Wow, Bridgett. This is very exciting. What pay range were you thinking of?"
>
> **Bridgett:** "Something between $35,000 and $40,000 per year."
>
> **Shane:** (In a neutral tone—not excited, not disappointed) "Hmmm…. $40,000…." (Shane counts to 10, silently, in his mind.)
>
> **Bridgett:** (After a few seconds of tense silence…) "Well, I could maybe bump that up a little. How about $42,000?"
>
> **Shane:** "$42,000…. Hmmm…" (another 10 seconds of silence).
>
> **Bridgett:** "$43,000 is about all I can offer. Will you take it?"
>
> **Shane:** "Let's set the pay part of the deal aside and talk about the other pieces of the offer."
>
> **Bridgett:** "Well, we offer a full benefits package. It's very good—vision, dental, the whole shebang."

Shane: "That's great!"

Bridgett: "And you'd qualify for two weeks of vacation the first year."

Shane: "In my current position, I've acquired close to four weeks each year. Could we get the vacation closer to four weeks?"

Bridgett: "Probably. Let me check on that."

Shane: "Is that it?"

Bridgett: (laughing) "We do offer a profit-sharing plan that our employees love. Most people on the team take home between 5 and 10 percent in additional pay from that plan each year."

Shane: "What about professional memberships?"

Bridgett: "We'd cover those that are reasonable, as well as send you to at least one conference each year."

Shane: "Wow, this all sounds great!"

Bridgett: "Good! So, will you take it?"

Shane: "I *am* very excited, but of course I need time to think about it. When would you need to have an answer from me?"

Bridgett: "How about by Monday?"

Shane: "That's fine. I'll call you then. And Bridgett, thanks for this opportunity!"

Shane used several powerful negotiating techniques in this example:

- He let Bridgett go first with the specifics related to money.

- He asked about a pay range, rather than a specific number, and began negotiating at the top of the range.

- He used the "repeat-it-thoughtfully-then-wait technique" for bumping up the salary, as in, "Hmm…. $40,000…."

- He repeated this technique until Bridgett seemed to reach her max.

- He pushed back respectfully when one aspect of the offer was unacceptable ("Could we get the vacation closer to four weeks?").

- Rather than say "Yes!" at the end of their discussion, Shane said, "…I need time to think about it. When would you need to hear from me?"

These strategies allow you, the potential new hire, to walk away from the initial negotiation with a pretty good offer—plus time to consider it carefully before accepting.

Come Back with a Counter Offer

After the early excitement of the offer has worn off, you'll have a chance to think things through more carefully. Is this what you really want? Are there any changes you want to propose? More money? A special request regarding your schedule? Now is the time to ask. This was Shane's counteroffer discussion:

Shane: "Bridgett, I've thought about your offer, and I have a few things I want to review with you."

Bridgett: "Let's hear them."

Shane: "First, I did a little research into competitive pay ranges for my specialty. According to our professional association's salary survey for last year, competitive pay falls between $40,000 and $50,000. Your offer of $43,000 is definitely in the ballpark. However, I'd be bringing 10 years of very successful experience to your organization. I'd like to see the pay in the upper half of the competitive range. Do you think we could work something out?"

Bridgett: "Well, our budget is tight, but how about this. I think I could bring you in at $45,000, and we could give you a pay review in 90 days. At that point—after you've had a chance to show us what you can do—I should be able to talk management into bumping your pay up to $47,000. I'll need to check on the $45,000, but if I can get it, would that work?"

Shane: "That part sounds good. Now, about the vacation. You said you would check on the four weeks. What did you find out?"

Bridgett: "I got the okay on that."

Shane: "Excellent! Would you be alright with me starting at the beginning of next month? I'd like to take a break between my current job and this new one."

Bridgett: "No problem. Anything else?"

Shane: "No, that all sounds good."

Bridgett: "Okay, let me confirm the new salary figure and I'll get back to you by the end of today."

Again, Shane made use of several effective negotiating techniques:

- He provided Bridgett with salary data that he'd researched from a credible source and requested that his pay reflect his experience.

- He was open to alternative options (waiting 90 days for a pay review), so that ultimately both sides could get what they wanted (Shane could make more money, and Bridgett could get Shane on her team).

- He confirmed that his request (for additional vacation) would be honored.

Shane was almost through! He was down to the last step: waiting for the final answer.

Wait... Then Celebrate!

Waiting for an approval on your negotiation request is one of the most nerve-wracking experiences known to man. When I was negotiating the deal for this book—an opportunity that would help me realize one of my biggest life dreams—I thought the anxiety was going to do me in before I ever had a chance to write my first sentence!

After several back-and-forth exchanges of information, requests, and offers, we were down to the final step. "I'll get back to you," my editor told me. And then I had to wait. To keep myself from going crazy, I used the following anxiety-management techniques:

- **Remind yourself that you have a lot to offer.** I reread my book proposal and reminded myself that it was a great product for the right publisher.

- **Review your options.** There were several (more than 100!) publishers to whom I could submit my proposal. Yes, I was very excited about *this* opportunity, but if we couldn't decide on a deal that worked for both of us, I did have other possibilities I could pursue.

- **Remember the aim of negotiation.** The purpose of negotiation is to allow both parties to arrive at a satisfactory agreement. What good would the deal be if both sides weren't happy? Keeping this in mind allowed me to be patient while waiting for the final answer.

- **Take into account that most of the things you fret over never come to pass.** I worried that the deal would dissolve, and I'd be left with nothing. But, as my grandmother used to say, "98 percent of what you worry about will never happen." I don't know if her figure is statistically correct, but I've learned that, most of the time, the things I agonize over never do become a reality.

- **Keep working toward your goal.** If for some reason this opportunity doesn't work out, you'll be much less disappointed if you have other possibilities in the works. Continue pursuing other options as your negotiations for this one play out.

When the deal *does* eventually come through, take time to celebrate. Mark the success with an event that recognizes all the work you put into the achievement. What was my celebration? I took my husband and some good friends out for margaritas!

Why It's Worth Doing

Negotiating is scary. It requires the negotiator (you) to ask for what you want, while risking losing what you've already been offered. Most people (Career Cowards especially) don't want to chance throwing away what they've already been presented. "It's better than nothing," they decide. "I'd better take it and run!"

Yet fairly quickly this creates a "lose-lose" situation for both the new hire and the employer. A few hours, days, or weeks later, the new hire grasps the reality of what he or she has accepted. "I'm really worth more!" they realize. "I should have negotiated more vacation time!" But instead of accepting responsibility for their own mistake of not negotiating a competitive package when an offer was made, they start to resent the employer. "It's not fair," the new hire grumbles. "The hiring manager should have paid me more! She should have asked how much vacation I wanted."

Then the hiring manager has an unhappy employee on her hands. One disappointment leads to another, and another, and within a short period of time, the relationship between the new hire and the manager deteriorates and fails.

Had the new hire thought through what he or she really wanted in the job offer, and requested it in a respectful way, the hiring manager would have had a chance to accommodate the new hire's needs. Their relationship would have started more successfully, and the prospect for creating a productive, long-term partnership would have been much more promising.

There's another valuable benefit of negotiating: It allows you to interact with your new employer on a challenging and important project immediately. As you exchange information about what each of you needs to make the deal work, you build trust between you. It's a *bonding* experience. By the time it's over, you truly feel like a team!

For several reasons, it's in your best interest, and in the interest of the hiring manager, to decide on and ask for what you really want when a job offer is made.

Career Champ Profile: Sylvia

Sylvia was negotiating the final details of an offer to become medical practice manager for a group of physicians. The partners had accepted her requests for salary, a built-in annual increase based on performance, and part ownership in the organization. Yet she was still waiting to hear whether they would agree to her final request: reorganizing the structure of the practice so that Sylvia would report to just one partner rather than seven.

Getting to this point in the negotiation had been challenging. After they'd made her an initial offer, Sylvia had created a list of 10 items she needed to negotiate. Then she met twice with the decision team to go over her wishes. But before discussing any of her items, Sylvia asked questions such as, "How did you decide to set things up this way?" and "What are you trying to accomplish with this method?" This allowed her to thoroughly understand their reasoning before requesting a change. And so far they'd been able to successfully work through every point on Sylvia's list—except for the request to reorganize.

The restructuring was Sylvia's "make it or break it" stipulation. She knew from past positions that if they didn't agree to change the reporting structure, it would create big problems for her down the line. Without it, it would just be better for Sylvia to pass on the offer.

Sylvia had been waiting for three days for their answer. In that time she'd reviewed her list of potential employers and checked in with her network about other possible jobs. Although she really hoped

she'd land this one position, she knew in her heart that other opportunities would come along if she wasn't able to work things out with
them.

Finally, the call came. "We finally agreed to reorganize," her contact
told her. "We'll put Brad in charge of the physicians, and you would
report directly to him. So, will you take the job?" "Absolutely!"
Sylvia said.

Core Courage Concept

Negotiating is one of the most nerve-wracking aspects of job searching. Yet Career Cowards who try it learn that negotiation builds
their confidence *and* results in a more trusting, productive relationship with their new employer. The key is in defining what you want
and communicating your requests respectfully to the hiring manager. Although it's scary, the payoffs are definitely worth the risk.

Confidence Checklist

☐ Learn when (and when not) to discuss money.

☐ Create your wish list.

☐ Negotiate the initial terms of the offer.

☐ Come back with a counter offer.

☐ Wait…then celebrate!

Chapter 17

Respond to and Recover from Rejection

After all of your hard work analyzing the position; developing What, How, and Proof stories; practicing your responses; and performing as well as you possibly could in the interview, you still didn't get an offer. And now you're left with nothing but disappointment, or so you think...

Risk It or Run From It?

- **Risk Rating:** Pretty low, but there is some risk involved with rejection, depending on how you handle it.

- **Payoff Potential:** Good things can come to those who lose. You'll be surprised!

- **Time to Complete:** From zero to 60 (minutes, I mean).

- **Bailout Strategy:** Skip it (but the pros always analyze their losses as well as their wins...).

- **The "20 Percent Extra" Edge:** Most people view a rejection as a dead end. Usually, however, there are several not-so-obvious (and often very productive) paths leading forward.

(continued)

(continued)

> • **"Go For It!" Bonus Activity:** Track all the positions you
> wanted but didn't get, and then stay in touch with the hiring
> managers, networking with them at least twice each year.
> Let them know that you're still very interested in becoming a
> part of their team.

How to Respond to and Recover from Rejection

You probably feel as if you want to throw this book out the window, considering all of the effort you put into interviewing that *still* didn't pay off. But don't throw in the towel (or this book) yet! Learning more about rejection and how to respond to it effectively will help you move more easily through all of the disappointments in life you're bound to encounter—and well-handled disappointments lead you faster to well-deserved successes.

Recover from the Rejection

Rejection is such a kick in the stomach, *especially* if you lost out on a job that you really wanted. There's no doubt that you're going to hurt for a while. Being disappointed is part of the process. By letting yourself feel disappointed (and not telling yourself to "just get over it!"), you'll be in better shape to handle whatever comes next.

In fact, wallowing in your frustrations for a while might actually help you find a job *faster*. One study showed that job searchers who wrote about their disappointments in journals for 20 minutes each day found work three times faster than those who didn't. Why? Because journaling provides a productive outlet for processing the feelings you experience during stressful situations. Moving your feelings from your mind onto paper allows you to clear those thoughts out of the way and think more strategically about the next best steps for yourself.

Your journal can be a handwritten record or a typewritten chronicle in a word-processing file. Whichever method you choose, keep the thoughts you write private (rather than in a public format such as a blog) so that you have complete freedom to air your frustrations. You don't want your annoyances or disappointments about a person or employer to come back to haunt you later on.

When you write each day, ask yourself, "What's going on in my mind—good and bad?" Then write down *everything* without editing yourself. Later you can choose to get rid of the evidence (throw away your notes or delete your file), but for now, let it all hang out.

Talking to someone you trust is another effective method for working through a rejection. As with journaling, talking with a supporter provides a productive outlet for your frustrations. Choose a confidante who believes in you, who is an excellent listener, and who doesn't have a hidden agenda. Because spouses are usually emotionally tied into your employment situation, they might not be the best choice. They might be thinking, "What are you doing wrong?" rather than, "How can I best support you?" Instead, seek out a loyal friend or a counselor and invest time talking about your feelings until you feel as though you've moved past the disappointment.

Learn What Rejection Really Means

It's almost impossible to not take rejection personally. Yet in most cases, the reasons you're not chosen for an opportunity have very little to do with you. Consider these common causes why people don't get the jobs they want:

1. The hiring manager had already picked someone before the interview process even started. Many interviews are conducted to meet the terms of an established hiring procedure. A company's human resources manual might state something like, "When openings become available within the company, they will be posted and subject to candidate selection through an interview process." That means that when a job becomes available, the hiring manager is required to interview candidates, even though he or she has *already decided who they want to hire.*

This happens frequently. And when a hiring manager already has a person in mind—someone they know from within their own company, or a person they've met through their network—you could interview like Super Employee and still not receive an offer. The decision was made long before you ever came on the scene.

2. The position was redefined during the interview process. In my experience, as many as one third of positions that my clients interview for wind up being redefined or scrapped altogether; the hiring manager changed his or her mind halfway through the process. Again, you could be "Super Employee" and it wouldn't make a lick of difference.

3. Another candidate had that "special something," and there was no way you could compete. You might have been highly qualified for a position, yet during the interview process the hiring manager discovered that another candidate spoke Swahili. Then he or she decided it would be handy to have that capability on their team. Again, it was nothing personal against you—but in the end you didn't get an offer.

The vast majority of the time, when you don't receive a job offer, *it's due to something completely unrelated to who you are and what you have to offer.* It's frustrating, but true. So what *can* you do to increase your chances of landing a great job after a rejection? Read on.

Put Things in Perspective

Okay, so you've wallowed in your disappointment for a while, and you're starting to see that the reason you didn't get this job is very likely due to something that was completely out of your control. Now what?

First, realize that interviewing is largely a numbers game: On average, you'll need to go through 10 interviews to receive one job offer.

Panic Point! "Ten interviews for one job offer? Yikes!" you might be thinking. Well, it's the reality. Working with thousands of clients, I've found the ten-interviews-to-one-job-offer ratio holds pretty true. So when you receive a rejection, rather than thinking, "I'm such a loser!" instead think, "One down, X more to go!"

Second, understand that if an opportunity didn't work out, it might have not been the best one for you, anyway. Countless times I've worked with clients who were passed up for one job, and then just a few weeks later interviewed and were offered another position that was *so much better for them.* You might feel desperate and frustrated now, but things are bound to take a turn in your favor eventually, as long as you persist effectively toward your goal.

Make Lemonade out of Lemons

Once the sting of the disappointment has faded a bit, you'll be able to look at the rejection more constructively. Can something positive come out of this experience? Absolutely! These action items will have you rolling again in no time.

Ask for Constructive Feedback

You didn't win the job, but you can still walk away with something valuable. Although not all hiring managers will provide criticism, some will, so it's worth asking. Phone or e-mail this request within one week of receiving a rejection:

> "Ms. Employer, thank you once again for interviewing me for your recent opening. It's the kind of position I hope to land one day. If you're willing, I'd appreciate any honest feedback you could give me on how to better present myself or how to strengthen my background so that in the future I will be more qualified for this kind of job. Please phone or e-mail me with any ideas, and I thank you in advance for your input."

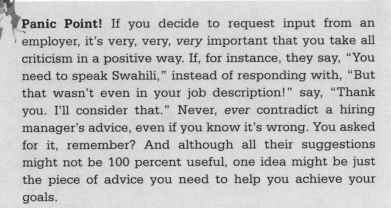

Panic Point! If you decide to request input from an employer, it's very, very, *very* important that you take all criticism in a positive way. If, for instance, they say, "You need to speak Swahili," instead of responding with, "But that wasn't even in your job description!" say, "Thank you. I'll consider that." Never, *ever* contradict a hiring manager's advice, even if you know it's wrong. You asked for it, remember? And although all their suggestions might not be 100 percent useful, one idea might be just the piece of advice you need to help you achieve your goals.

Wait for a Second Chance

Remember that as many as 40 percent of new hires don't work out within the first six months. The new employee might end up lacking the skills necessary for the job or not getting along well with the team. Whatever the cause, hiring managers become frustrated with, fire, or pawn off 4 in 10 of their new hires in the first 180 days.

This creates a golden opportunity for you to step in where another employee is failing. Check back with a potential employer at three months, six months, nine months, and so on, to say

> "Hello, Ms. Employer. It's [YOUR NAME], just calling to say hello and to check in with you about any upcoming opportunities in your organization. When I interviewed with you a few months ago, I was especially excited about the possibility of working with you and helping [ORGANIZATION NAME] achieve its goals. Please keep me in mind. I can be reached at [PHONE NUMBER]."

View the Job You Didn't Get as a Model for the One You Want

What kind of position was it, and in which type of company? Now do your homework to find out the names of similar businesses in your target geographic area. Research the decision makers' names as well, and then contact them directly to request a chance to introduce yourself. This way, you'll be the person the hiring manager has already decided to hire when the *next* opening becomes available.

Why It's Worth Doing

Rejection is a fact of life. We all know the story of Abraham Lincoln's many rejections before he won his job as president. But, thankfully, he persisted and the right man eventually landed in the right job!

There are many, many opportunities available in the job market. Yet most people get frustrated and throw in the towel way too soon, missing out on positions that would be ideal for them.

Learning how to handle and move on from rejection is a skill that will allow you to succeed long after others have given up. Go ahead…be frustrated for a while. Journal or talk it through with a supporter until you're past the worst of it, and then brush yourself off and jump back in. Sheer persistence—waiting out the average of 10 interviews it will take to finally receive an offer—combined with a few smart-to-do steps like keeping in touch with the hiring manager and introducing yourself to other decision makers in the industry, will eventually provide you what you want: a great job!

Career Champ Profile: Savannah

Savannah was frustrated. She'd interviewed for seven positions in the last two months and hadn't received one offer. As a marketing specialist for medical offices, there seemed to be several openings—but not one was offered to Savannah. Each rejection was difficult, yet Savannah did her best to remember that it would take an average of 10 interviews to land a great job, and she needed to keep on plugging.

After every interview, she analyzed her performance and worked on ways to improve her presentation. She'd even taken a database class after one hiring manager told her it would help her to be more marketable.

But the last rejection had been especially painful. Savannah had cultivated a relationship with the hiring manager over several months, networking with him every few weeks, and putting together special reports to help him in his business planning.

"He practically owed me that job!" Savannah grumbled to me in a meeting after she'd received the bad news. "Would it have been ideal for you?" I asked, encouraging her to talk about her disappointment. "Well…yes and no," she said. She then went on to explain that this last position would have involved more direct sales than Savannah liked. "I would have done it, but it wouldn't have been my favorite part."

Savannah was pretty down for a few days. She treated herself to a few tearjerker movies and called her girlfriends to share her tale of woe. On the following Monday she was ready to try again. "I have some people I can contact at other medical offices," she told me. "I met them at a recent conference. I'd been meaning to call them, and now is probably a good time for me to follow through."

Melanie, the first person Savannah contacted, didn't remember her right away. But after reminding her about the class they took together at the conference, Melanie warmed up and agreed to meet with Savannah on Friday. Almost as soon as they began talking, Melanie told Savannah about an opportunity opening up at her office. "We need someone to develop relationships with referral sources in the community. We also need someone to handle training in basic office procedures for our new employees. Any chance you have experience in that area?" It turned out that Savannah did have a training background, and Melanie said that she'd be organizing the hiring process for that job in the next few weeks.

The following Sunday, Savannah saw a posting in the Help Wanted section advertising the position. Savannah submitted her resume directly to Melanie, and Melanie set up an appointment for three days later. When they met, Savannah was ready with several What, How, and Proof stories that backed up her expertise in building referral relationships and training employees. The interview went great; all the interviews Savannah had gone through for other positions really helped her polish her presentation skills.

Melanie called and offered Savannah the job the next morning. Later that same day, when Savannah called to tell me the good news, she was practically giddy. "I *love* training! I used to have a job where training was a part of my responsibilities, but I haven't been able to be a trainer in my last two positions. This job is *so* much better for me than the last job would have been. I'm so glad I wasn't offered it!"

Core Courage Concept

Of all the interview steps you've worked on to this point, this is probably the hardest to do and master. Because rejection is *so* painful, it can feel as though it would just be better to crawl in a hole and give up. Yet you know there's a better job out there for you. Wading through a few rejections is just part of getting to that opportunity. You're strong…you *can* do it…and it will definitely be worth it in the end.

Confidence Checklist

☐ Recover from the rejection.

☐ Learn what rejection really means.

☐ Put things in perspective.

☐ Make lemonade out of lemons.

Chapter 18

Handling Awkward Interview Situations

In a perfect world, interviews would progress without a hitch. Yet who lives in a perfect world? Complications are bound to arise. Expand your expertise by learning how to respond to a variety of interviewing challenges.

Risk It or Run From It?

- **Risk Rating:** Low to high…depending on the topic and how you respond.

- **Payoff Potential:** Could make the difference between a "no" and a "go!"

- **Time to Complete:** Typically just a minute or two.

- **Bailout Strategy:** Blunder forward in ignorance.

- **The "20 Percent Extra" Edge:** Special situations call for special treatment. A little extra knowledge will help you navigate challenging situations more successfully.

- **"Go For It!" Bonus Activity:** Work with a supporter to role-play your response to the awkward situation affecting you. The practice will increase your confidence and improve your results.

How to Handle Awkward Interview Situations

Should you tell your boss you're interviewing? Tell the interviewer you're pregnant? Are you being discriminated against for age? And how should you handle multiple interviews and offers? These situations can seem awkward and stressful, yet sorting them out typically takes just a solid strategy and a little common sense.

Juggle Interviews with Your Current Job

"Should I tell my boss that I'm looking for another job? I feel as if I should!" Many job searchers wonder whether they should tell their boss that they're job searching. They want to alleviate their guilt by coming clean with the news, plus give their boss a heads-up that they'll eventually need to be replaced.

Although you might feel as though you're doing your boss a favor, it's actually a bad idea to let him or her in on your plan to change jobs. For now, your future is still unclear. You might land a new job next week, next month, or next year, or you might ultimately decide that you don't want to change jobs at all. Yet by telling your boss, "I'll probably be moving on sometime in the near future..." it puts *him* in an awkward state of limbo. Should he keep you in the loop, especially if you wind up going to work for a competitor? Should he assign you important projects, considering that you might not be there to finish them? Should he start interviewing other people now?

Consider what happened to Keith when he attempted to switch from his position as an assistant football coach at a college to a job as a pharmaceutical sales rep. In March, when he made the decision to change careers, he decided to tell his boss. His boss was disappointed, but said that he wished Keith the best. Then, for the next *12 months*, Keith searched and interviewed for jobs. He had several first and second interviews, but no offers for over a year. Meanwhile, back at the university, Keith's life had become miserable. It was obvious that his boss and coworkers viewed him as a "short-timer," and he was frequently left out of conversations, activities, and decisions.

Eventually Keith did get a job as a pharmaceutical sales rep, but the experience helped him learn a valuable lesson: "I wish I'd waited until I had a job offer, and then given two weeks' notice, rather than telling my boss so early on. It would have been better for me to live with the guilt than to suffer through the cold-shoulder treatment. Plus, I realize now that my situation made things awkward for them."

Manage Age Concerns

"I think I'm being discriminated against because of age." This is a common concern among job searchers aged 40 and over. They interview for a job, don't get it, and then wonder if it had something to do with their age. Maybe it did, maybe it didn't, yet attempting to discover the truth of the situation would involve an expensive and lengthy investigation. As a job searcher seeking an attractive position, do you really want to devote your time, energy, and resources to a legal dispute with a potential employer? Talk about limiting your chances for the future!

As a 40+ job searcher, you can improve your attractiveness to an employer through the following means:

- **Present a competitive skill set.** Being experienced and wise isn't enough. And "I'll learn what I need to know when I get the job" is an attitude that might keep you from getting your toe in the door at all. If the positions that interest you specify knowledge of certain technology or techniques, be sure they're a part of your skill set, taking any necessary classes or certification programs to get up to speed. Regardless of your age, your qualifications need to be competitive.

- **Include no more than 15 to 20 years of history on your resume.** Otherwise, the decision maker might assume that you're "too old," "too expensive," or "too set in your ways," judging simply by what he or she sees on paper. Give your resume a chance to successfully land you an interview.

- **If you're excited about an opportunity, show it.** Enthusiasm is attractive at any age.

Having observed the results of thousands of interview candidates, I can report that age appears to be a minimal issue, if one at all. Candidates of all ages, from early 20s to 70+, are able to successfully secure positions through effective and persistent promotion of their qualifications and talents.

Address Your Pregnancy

Pregnancy—a joyous event, but it can cause complications during interviews. And what you reveal about your condition is directly related to where you are in your process.

If it's not yet obvious that you're expecting, keep mum about your condition until *after* you've received a job offer and *before* you accept it. That's the ideal time to review your plans and needs.

If it *is* obvious that you're expecting, you'll need to address the issue early in the interview process. Otherwise, imagine the hiring manager's surprise and potential panic upon encountering a candidate heavy with child: "Oh goodness, she's pregnant! When is she due? For how long will she be out on maternity leave? Will she be able to juggle a baby *and* this job? Should I call an ambulance *now?*" The hiring manager might be so surprised that he or she won't be able to calm down enough to focus on your true potential for the position.

As with age (or race, or gender), pregnancy shouldn't be an issue in interviewing. Yet because of a hiring manager's potential concerns, it's in your best interest to comment on your obvious pregnancy early in the interview process. For instance, *after* you've been contacted to arrange an interview, and *before* you show up for the meeting, share this message with the hiring manager:

> "Ms. Hiring Manager, I just want to give you a heads up that when we meet, you'll see that I'm expecting. I look forward to

discussing my plans regarding my pregnancy when we get together."

When you do meet, share your strategy for maternity leave and other related accommodations early in the interview, opening the conversation this way:

"Ms. Hiring Manager, I'd like to take a minute to talk with you about my maternity leave and child-care plans as they would relate to how I would handle this job. Is this a good time?"

Then communicate your strategy. For instance, when Isla was eight months pregnant, she interviewed for a customer service manager position. This was her second child, so Isla was able to provide the hiring manager with detailed What, How, and Proof stories about how she'd successfully handled maternity leave and child care for her first child, with the intention of using the same system for her second. The hiring manager's concerns were addressed, and he offered Isla the job.

Orchestrate Timing for Interviews and Offers

Until you master control of the universe (and I'm still working on this one...), you'll occasionally run into poor timing issues when it comes to interviewing. Let's say, for example, that you've been offered a job and then you receive a call to interview for another position—one that looks as if it could be an even *better* fit for you. You'd first need to determine whether the first offer is even worth considering, depending on your career goals. If it is a decent position, and you don't want to turn it down until you've checked out the other possibility, buy yourself some time with this kind of statement:

"Mr. Hiring Manager, I have a personal matter that I need to resolve in the next two weeks. Would it be possible for me to postpone giving you my decision until [DATE]?"

If you're pressed to provide details, say,

"I feel that this matter is one that is better kept to myself. I hope you can respect my privacy on this issue."

Although you don't want to communicate that another job might be more appealing to you than theirs, you might be able to stretch out the timing enough to allow you the chance to consider both opportunities.

Deal with More than One Offer at a Time

Lucky you—you're wanted by more than one employer! It can feel great to be in such high demand. It can also be very stressful. Which job should you choose, and how will you decide?

Begin by looking at your career wish list. What's truly important to you? Is it the responsibilities, manager, team, purpose, location, money, potential for advancement, or something else? A prioritized list of your career goals will help you evaluate the actual potential of each offer.

If it helps in your decision-making, request further meetings with the hiring manager or team members to gain a better understanding of the scope and challenges of the opportunity. In most cases, once you've gathered enough information, the choice will become clear.

If, in the end, you're trying to decide between two positions and pay *is* a deciding factor, you can negotiate one opportunity against the other:

> "Ms. Hiring Manager, I've been offered another job with pay that is slightly more in line with my worth in the market. My first choice would be to work for you. I wanted to check with you on the chance that your company could match or improve on my other offer."

Panic Point! Be very cautious in choosing one job over another based on salary alone. Additional money rarely makes people happier. If the position doesn't satisfy your other priorities, you'll soon discover that the extra money isn't enough to keep you satisfied for the long term.

Why It's Worth Doing

Although we might wish that interviews would unfold without biases or complications, inevitably interesting and challenging issues find their way into our lives. You can't control the opinion of the interviewer, yet you *can* control how you respond.

Typically, our first instinct is to react with fear and panic: "Oh no! I'm too old / pregnant / stressed to handle this successfully." Yet in most cases, when we look at the circumstances more objectively, we discover that by communicating our plans and hopes clearly, and by making reasonable requests, situations that once seemed too complicated to sort out unravel themselves easily.

There's another, even better bonus that comes from learning how to respond effectively to awkward situations: We build confidence in our abilities. "Wow, I solved this sticky problem successfully. I'll most likely be able to solve the next problem, too!" And by solving one problem after another, we're able to consistently overcome challenges and move forward in our careers.

Career Champ Profile: Vicki

Vicki had just turned 53 when her employer laid her off. She'd hoped that this purchasing position with a technology manufacturing company would be her last before retirement.

"Won't other companies think I'm too old?" she asked me nervously during our career counseling session. "Some might," I told her honestly, "but others will think you're perfect for their needs."

Despite her concerns, Vicki jumped bravely into a job search. She updated and overhauled her resume, removing dates from her education and showing only the last 15 years of her work history. She took a two-day advanced-skills course on a popular industry software program. She researched companies that were appealing to her and once again became active in professional associations.

It took only a few months for interviews to begin coming Vicki's way. A classmate in her software course arranged for Vicki to interview for a position opening at her company. A colleague Vicki knew through a professional group tipped her off to a job opportunity with a new company in town. And a networking contact that Vicki had recently reconnected with introduced her to a recruiter who was filling a purchasing position.

"I'm too old for all these interviews!" Vicki told me, laughing, during one of our interview practice sessions. "But my age doesn't seem to be getting in the way, does it?" She was dressed in a gorgeous deep-purple suit with a white blouse that accentuated her beautifully styled gray hair. Rather than old, she looked sharp and savvy.

It wasn't long before Vicki accepted an offer for a position that paid 10 percent more than her last job. When I saw her a few months later, she said, "It's funny, I thought I wanted to stay in my old job until I retired. But I'm having *so much fun* in this new position, I can't image it ending in just 10 years or so. I may want to keep on working!"

Core Courage Concept

Awkward situations are especially intimidating. "What if this happens? Or that?" Usually, however, by taking a deep breath, gathering information, using common sense, and treating others with respect, you can sort through and handle situations that at one time seemed impossible to solve—and you'll find new belief in yourself along the way.

Confidence Checklist

- ☐ Juggle interviews with your current job.
- ☐ Manage age concerns.
- ☐ Address your pregnancy.
- ☐ Orchestrate timing for interviews and offers.
- ☐ Deal with more than one offer at a time.

Chapter 19

Analyze Your Own Interviewing Strengths and Weaknesses

You've come a long way from where you began as a cowardly interview candidate, afraid and unsure of how to present yourself to make progress toward your career goals. You've tried new things and taken risks to break old patterns and achieve better results. You should feel very proud of yourself. But is it enough? Could you become even more skilled at interviewing? This chapter will help you uncover opportunities for achieving even better interview results.

Risk It or Run From It?

- **Risk Rating:** No risk. Just a chance to recognize your accomplishments and scope out additional possibilities to grow.

- **Payoff Potential:** Sizeable. It's a painless yet powerful process that can help you become an even more effective interviewer.

- **Time to Complete:** Three to five minutes.

(continued)

(continued)

- **Bailout Strategy:** Skip it. If you've done a thorough job of completing the exercises in this book, and if you're getting great results from your interviews, you're probably in pretty good shape, anyway.

- **The "20 Percent Extra" Edge:** Celebrate your strengths and then make adjustments to your weak points. Soon your interview skills will pull you even farther ahead of the pack.

- **"Go For It!" Bonus Activity:** In addition to analyzing your performance based on the general statements included in this assessment, scrutinize your outcomes for the individual activities described in each chapter, looking out for other ways to improve your results.

How to Identify Your Interviewing Strengths and Weaknesses

You've completed quite a journey, from targeting and landing interviews for jobs you want; to preparing, practicing, and responding to the interviews you've had. Chances are you've accomplished more than you realize. Congratulations! Your hard work deserves to be recognized (by you, if by nobody else!).

You might also be looking for ways to further refine and improve your interviewing skills. Where should you focus your efforts? The following assessment and development plan will help you review your successes and capitalize on opportunities for continued growth.

Complete the "How'd You Do?" Interview Results Assessment

Read the following statements and evaluate your results on a 0 to 10 scale, with 0 being "I didn't really do this at all," 10 being "I put 100 percent effort into this activity," and a 1 to 9 rating indicating your actual amount of effort, from 10 percent to 90 percent.

1. "I defined the type of job I'd really love to have, including 3 to 10 specific aspects of my ideal work. I set aside my 'It'll never

happen for me!' fears and created an inspiring picture of the career I want to achieve. From there, I researched potential job options using resources such as www.monster.com and used this information to create targeted resumes and identify possible employers. I then pursued interviews through effective job searching techniques. Finally, I began the process of visualizing myself as a successful interviewer." *(Topics addressed in chapter 1.)*

"How'd You Do?" Rating: _____

Ideas for additional action steps and next-round improvements:

_____

_____

2. "I gained a better understanding of the challenges hiring managers face related to interviewing and hiring a new employee. Knowing more about a decision maker's priorities and frustrations helped me apply for jobs and pursue interviews more successfully." *(Topics addressed in chapter 2.)*

"How'd You Do?" Rating: _____

Ideas for additional action steps and next-round improvements:

_____

_____

3. "I followed up on my job applications, contacting potential employers through e-mail or phone up to three times, following a script that would help me set up more interviews." *(Topics addressed in chapter 3.)*

"How'd You Do?" Rating: _____

Ideas for additional action steps and next-round improvements:

_____

_____

4. "To begin preparing for an interview, I focused on a specific job and analyzed the ad or description to identify the three to five most important key skill areas for the position. I then used resources I have, such as resumes, performance reviews, and school transcripts, to brainstorm at least five examples from my past that provide evidence of my abilities in each of the position's key skill areas. I pushed through my 'I have no experience in this area' and 'this instance isn't important enough' fears and listed several potential examples to use in my interview preparation." *(Topics addressed in chapter 4.)*

"How'd You Do?" Rating: _____

Ideas for additional action steps and next-round improvements:

_____

_____

5. "I learned the value of preparing What, How, and Proof stories, and picked one of my examples to develop into one of these three-part answers. I then worked with several of my examples until I'd created a powerful Success Database of What, How, and Proof stories to use in interviews." *(Topics addressed in chapter 5.)*

"How'd You Do?" Rating: _____

Ideas for additional action steps and next-round improvements:

_____

_____

6. "To better understand my potential employer's priorities, needs, and challenges, I researched data about the company

where I'd be interviewing, including information about key managers and employees, competitors, and industry trends." *(Topics addressed in chapter 6.)*

"How'd You Do?" Rating: _____

Ideas for additional action steps and next-round improvements:

_____

_____

7. "So that I would be comfortable and confident telling my favorite What, How, and Proof stories in interviews, I read through, practiced, timed, and refined them until they were interesting and easy to understand, could be conveyed in one or two minutes, and were comfortable for me to tell, even in stressful situations." *(Topics addressed in chapter 7.)*

"How'd You Do?" Rating: _____

Ideas for additional action steps and next-round improvements:

_____

_____

8. "I developed and practiced excellent responses to 'tell me about yourself' and 'describe your strengths and weaknesses' questions by brainstorming, analyzing, and choosing engaging and appropriate information to share. I then practiced them extensively so that I could share them easily in interviews, helping to keep my confidence high and my performance strong." *(Topics addressed in chapter 8.)*

"How'd You Do?" Rating: _____

Ideas for additional action steps and next-round improvements:

_____

_____

9. "So that I could perform better in traditional interviews, I learned more about how they work and developed and practiced answers to several popular traditional-interview questions. I also learned how to respond to sensitive or inappropriate questions, including what to say about working for a difficult employer, as well as how to handle questions about career mistakes and disappointments." *(Topics addressed in chapter 9.)*

   "How'd You Do?" Rating: _____

   Ideas for additional action steps and next-round improvements:

   _____

   _____

10. "I learned about nontraditional interview formats, including techniques for how to handle myself well in behavioral, situational, technical, and phone interviews. I also developed and practiced potential answers to behavioral questions so that I'll be better equipped to handle challenging 'give me an example of a time...' questions." *(Topics addressed in chapter 10.)*

    "How'd You Do?" Rating: _____

    Ideas for additional action steps and next-round improvements:

    _____

    _____

11. "To build my belief in myself inside *and* out, I took a hard look at my self-talk and how I present myself to others. I then polished my handshake, eye contact, smile, and listening skills, and learned techniques for keeping my confidence high even when I'm stressed. I also evaluated my appearance, including

my face, hair, grooming, and clothing, and took steps to look my best for interviews." *(Topics addressed in chapter 11.)*

"How'd You Do?" Rating: ____

Ideas for additional action steps and next-round improvements:

_____

_____

12. "I set myself up to make an excellent first impression in the first few minutes of an interview. I scoped out the location ahead of time and prepared the materials I'd need to take, such as copies of my resume, business cards, a notepad, a portfolio, and my Accomplishments listing. I then mastered my initial greeting and memorized some small-talk topics." *(Topics addressed in chapter 12.)*

    "How'd You Do?" Rating: ____

    Ideas for additional action steps and next-round improvements:

    _____

    _____

13. "I learned how to handle myself with confidence throughout the interview, including what to do when I can't think of an answer, how to help myself recall a good example when my mind draws a blank, how to gracefully reply to inappropriate questions, and what to do if I really mess up on an answer." *(Topics addressed in chapter 13.)*

    "How'd You Do?" Rating: ____

    Ideas for additional action steps and next-round improvements:

    _____

    _____

14. "When it comes to wrapping up interviews effectively, I've learned how to make sure that I've shared the most important information about myself and how to respond to the question, 'why should we hire you?' I've also developed a list of appropriate questions for the interviewer, and I know how to leave the interview with a clear understanding of what will happen next in the process." *(Topics addressed in chapter 14.)*

    "How'd You Do?" Rating: _____

    Ideas for additional action steps and next-round improvements:

    _____

    _____

15. "I'm now skilled at analyzing how I performed in an interview and developing an action plan for improving my results in the next one. I also know how to wrap up any loose ends, prepare and send a thank-you note, and follow up with the hiring manager to keep the process moving forward smoothly." *(Topics addressed in chapter 15.)*

    "How'd You Do?" Rating: _____

    Ideas for additional action steps and next-round improvements:

    _____

    _____

16. "When a job offer comes through, I have a strategy for evaluating the offer to determine whether it's a good match for what I want. I also know how to negotiate any items that I want to change, including pay. Additionally, I now know when it's finally okay to say, 'yes, I'll take it!' to the offer." *(Topics addressed in chapter 16.)*

    "How'd You Do?" Rating: _____

Ideas for additional action steps and next-round improvements:

_____

_____

17. "If I receive a rejection, I have a plan for dealing with it, putting it in perspective, getting feedback on how I can improve my chances next time, and moving on to the next opportunity." *(Topics addressed in chapter 17.)*

    "How'd You Do?" Rating: _____

    Ideas for additional action steps and next-round improvements:

    _____

    _____

18. "When awkward situations come up related to things such as telling my current boss that I'm job searching and addressing things like pregnancy, age, timing for multiple interviews, and deciding between more than one offer, I am armed with techniques and scripts for responding to them successfully." *(Topics addressed in chapter 18.)*

    "How'd You Do?" Rating: _____

    Ideas for additional action steps and next-round improvements:

    _____

    _____

Calculate Your Results and Then Make Adjustments

When you're finished, give yourself a standing ovation for your higher (8+) ratings. You've worked hard, pushing through your fears to make progress toward your career goals. Even though you were scared at times, you took some risks and accomplished some impressive results.

Now you'll need to decide whether you want to put additional effort into raising your scores on any items with a lower rating (anything with a score of 7 or lower is a good candidate for improvement). Think about choosing one area at a time to tackle, and then move on to the next, until you're satisfied with all of your results. If you tried a recommended activity and got poor results, consider trying a different approach next time. It might also help to get additional support through a friend or counselor or to motivate yourself with a different reward. Ultimately, you want to break ineffective interviewing patterns and achieve better results.

Why It's Worth Doing

A step-by-step analysis of your interviewing strengths and weaknesses arms you with valuable feedback about what you're doing well and where you could stand to get better. Knowing exactly where to funnel your interviewing efforts helps you move toward your career goals faster and more easily.

Career Champ Profile: Clayton

Clayton had come a long way toward improving his effectiveness in interviews. When he started the process, he'd been stuck in job he hated for three years, primarily because he was too scared to interview for a new one. As he learned techniques for improving his interview skills, however, Clayton's confidence grew and he decided to risk applying for a few jobs. Within three months he'd landed four interviews.

Using the interviewing techniques described in this book, Clayton mastered a strong set of self-presentation skills and began feeling better about his ability to make good eye contact and engage in small talk with the hiring managers who had once seemed so terrifying to him. He also discovered that he especially loved the process of analyzing a position's key skill areas and developing several What, How, and Proof stories as evidence of his ability to perform successfully in a specific job.

Yet when he took a hard look at his effort and results, he realized that he hadn't been devoting enough time or effort to practicing his interview responses. His busy home, filled with a wife and two small children, made it difficult for him to find a private place to rehearse his answers.

Determined put in more practice time, Clayton began taking the family dog on walks down a quiet wooded path, carrying along his list of What, How, and Proof stories. He practiced his stories over and over as they walked along. The more he walked and practiced, the more confident Clayton felt about describing his strengths. The dog seemed pretty impressed, too.

In his next interview, Clayton noticed a huge difference in his self-belief. His What, How, and Proof stories flowed more smoothly, and instead of worrying about remembering the details of his stories, he found that he was able to relax and talk easily with the hiring manager. Even better, the extra practice paid off. Clayton landed the job.

Core Courage Concept

It takes nerve to dissect how you're really doing in interviews. Who likes to look at their flaws, anyway? Yet often, just a few small changes can lead to big leaps in results, so maybe it's worth the risk after all. Willing to try? Then take a deep breath and go for it!

Confidence Checklist

☐ Complete the "How'd You Do?" interview results assessment.

☐ Calculate your results and then make adjustments.

Know Exactly What to Say: Your Scripts Toolbox

L ooking for help with what to say related to interviewing? The following scripts and examples will give you some great ideas, from setting up job interviews all the way through to accepting an offer.

Scripts for Before the Interview

The following scripts are helpful for creating and scheduling job interview opportunities.

To Help Create an Opportunity for an Interview When No Specific Job Is Advertised

Mail a letter and resume requesting a chance to introduce yourself, even though no specific job is advertised, and then follow up:

> "I just wanted to make sure you received my information successfully. I'd like the chance to meet with you to introduce myself and see if there are ways that we can support each other in the future. If I don't hear from you in the next day or so, I'll phone you to make sure this e-mail got through."

To Follow Up on an Application for an Advertised Job

What to say when you follow up via e-mail or phone on a resume you submitted for an advertised job:

First Attempt:

> "I am following up on a resume I submitted for the [JOB TITLE] position you currently have open. This position appears to be a great match for my skills and background. I want to confirm that my materials have been received, and to find out what happens from here. You can contact me at [E-MAIL OR PHONE]. If I haven't heard from you in the next day or so, I will follow up with you to make sure this message was received successfully. I look forward to talking with you soon."

Second Attempt: "Just checking back on my message from yesterday. You can contact me at [PHONE or E-MAIL], or I'll try you again in a day or so."

Third (and Final) Attempt:

> "We seem to be having a hard time connecting, but I wanted to try reaching you one more time. I would very much like to talk to you about the [JOB TITLE] position you currently have open. I can be reached at [YOUR CONTACT INFO], and I'm hopeful I'll hear from you soon. Whether or not we get to talk, I wish you the best in finding the right person for this opportunity."

To Schedule a More Convenient Time for a Phone Interview

How to sidestep a surprise phone interview when you're not ready for it:

> "I would love to talk with you further about this position, but I need to leave for an appointment in a minute. I could meet with you tomorrow or Thursday. Would one of those days work for you, or should we choose another day?"

To Postpone Discussion About Pay Too Early in the Process

What to say when you're asked about your pay requirements before the first interview has been scheduled:

> "Ms. Interviewer, I would feel more comfortable discussing pay after we've determined that I'm the right person for the job. I hope you're okay with that."

What to say if you're pressed further for pay requirement information:

> "It sounds as if you're working within a certain pay range. Since you're familiar with your company's pay scale, how about if you tell me the range you're thinking of, and I'll let you know whether it sounds fair to me."

What to say if the interviewer refuses to let you off the hook about pay requirements:

> "For this type of position, as researched in a variety of up-to-date sources, a pay range between \$X and \$Y is competitive."

To Help You Gather Company Information Before an Interview

How to ask your networking contacts for information about a company or people you'll be interviewing with:

> "Bob, next Monday I'm interviewing for a job at *Experienced Cruiser* magazine. Julie Smith, Kyle Green, and Martha Gephardt are on the interview team. I'd like to gather as much information as possible about the company, their projects, and the team. Do you have any information to share, or could you recommend anybody I should contact who might know more?"

To Address Being Pregnant as You're Scheduling Your Interview

What to tell a hiring manager before your interview if you're visibly pregnant:

"Ms. Hiring Manager, I just want to give you a heads up that when we meet, you'll see that I'm expecting. I look forward to discussing my plans regarding my pregnancy when we get together."

Scripts for During the Interview

These scripts will help you handle yourself well in a variety of situations during an interview.

To Make a Positive First Impression

What to say to the interviewer when he or she greets you:

"Hello, Mr./Ms. (fill in their last name). Thank you for the opportunity to meet with you today."

What questions to ask to when making small talk:

- Are you from this area originally?
- How long have you worked here?
- Has the company always been in this location?
- What do you like to do for fun?
- Any exciting adventures or trips coming up for you?

To Handle Sensitive Questions Successfully

How to respond to questions about sensitive topics, such as working for a difficult employer or boss:

"There are certain details about that situation that I believe are better not to discuss. I hope you'll respect my privacy on that topic."

How to respond to an inappropriate question about religion or family:

"I hope you won't mind, but I have a policy of not discussing personal matters unless they relate directly to the position."

To Handle Questions When Your Mind Goes Blank

What to say when you draw a blank on a question and need more time to think of an answer:

"That's a really good question. May I have just a minute to think about it?"

What to say if by the end of the interview, you still don't have an answer to a question you asked for a postponement on:

"Mr. Interviewer, I had hoped to have an answer to this question by now, but I don't. I would like to get back to you with a response by tomorrow. Would you prefer that I phone you or send it via e-mail?"

What to say when you need to look at your resume or Accomplishments list to help you recall an answer to a question:

"I believe there's a good example of my experience right here. Let me locate it for you…."

What to say if you absolutely, positively don't know the answer to a question:

"Mr. Interviewer, I don't know the answer to that question. But the way I would find an answer would be…."

Then talk about what you would do to find the information you'd need, such as contacting an expert or looking up information in a reference book.

What to say if the question they ask you doesn't make sense:

"Could you please rephrase that in a different way?"

To Respond Effectively to Questions You're Asked

How to use an "answer sandwich" format for answers to questions you're asked, so that you stay on track:

First slice of bread: "So, Mr. Interviewer, you want to know about my experience in (fill in topic)…."

Middle of the sandwich: Give your answer.

Second slice of bread: "So that is some information about my experience with (fill in topic)."

What to say if you don't have experience with the topic presented in the question, but you do have background in an area that's similar:

"Although I don't have direct experience with what you're describing, I do have experience with something very similar...."

What to say if you totally mess up on an interview answer:

"I'd like a chance to answer this one again if I may...."

Or

"I'm really sorry. I'm just a little nervous. I hope you'll forgive me."

To Respond to Questions About Pay During an Interview

How to respond to "What kind of money do you want to make?":

"I'd feel more comfortable discussing that once we've determined that I'm the right person for the job. I hope you're okay with that."

What to say if you're pressed further to provide information about pay:

"Since you know the company's pay scales, how about if you tell me what range you are thinking about, and I'll let you know if that sounds like it's in my ballpark?"

What to say if the interviewer asks you, at any time during the interview, "Would you take the job for $X?":

"Ms. Interviewer, are you offering me a job?":

To Answer "Why Should We Hire You?"

What to say when you're asked "why should we hire you?":

"Well, Mr. Interviewer, I'd be the right person for the job because I have proven experience succeeding with responsibilities just like those required for this position. For instance, one time I...."

Or

"Mr. Interviewer, as you've stated, you're looking for someone with strengths in the key skill areas of A, B, and C. Through the examples I've shared, I've demonstrated my ability to succeed in the most important aspects of this job."

Or

> "Mr. Interviewer, I know I can do a great job for you, and I'd love the opportunity to prove it."

To Respond to "What Questions Do You Have for Me?"

What to say when you're asked "do you have any questions for me?":

"Yes, I've written some down…" (and choose from the following list):

- What do you see as this position's greatest challenge at the present?
- Why is this position open at this time?
- What are your immediate objectives and priorities for this position?
- What characteristics do you value most in an employee?
- Where does this position fit within your organization?
- What projects do you need done, and in what order?
- Please describe the culture of the company (for example, dress, energy level, and so on).
- How is performance measured, and how is successful performance rewarded?
- Please tell me about the training I would receive.
- How does this organization support professional growth?
- What does the company hope to accomplish in the next few years?
- If you could wave a magic wand and have the perfect person for this position, what would they be like?
- What could I do for you so that this time next year, your boss would think we're both geniuses?

To Wrap Up the Interview Effectively

What to say when the interview is almost over and you realize you forgot to share some important information about your background:

"Mr. Interviewer, I just thought of an example from my background that is particularly relevant to the skills needed for this position. May I share it?"

What to say at the end of the interview, to make it clear that you want the job:

"I would love to have this position and to be a part of your team."

What to say at the end of the interview, to find out what will happen next:

"Mr. Interviewer, what will be your next step in this process? And when can I expect to hear something?"

Scripts for After the Interview

These scripts will help you continue to make career progress after an interview.

To Follow Up After a Job Interview

First Attempt: What to say when you follow up with a hiring manager after an interview:

"Hello, Mr. Interviewer. This is Julie Brown. When I interviewed with you last Thursday, you mentioned that a next step would be decided by Tuesday of this week. I wanted to check in with you about the status of the hiring process. I'm still very interested in the position. I can be reached at (953) 555-1212."

Second Attempt:

"Hello, Mr. Interviewer. It's Julie Brown again. I left a message yesterday, and I wanted to make sure you'd received it. You mentioned that a next step in your hiring process would most likely be decided by this time. I'm still very excited about your opportunity, and I look forward to hearing from you about where we go from here. I can be contacted at (953) 555-1212 or through my e-mail at juliebrown@email.com. Thank you for your time."

Third Attempt:

> "Hello, Mr. Interviewer. It's Julie Brown again. I'm guessing that you must be extremely busy or away from the office. Please know that I'm still very interested in the position and would love the chance to work with you and your organization. My phone number is (953) 555-1212, and I'll wait to hear from you. If for some reason I wasn't selected for the job, I wish you and the company great success with the person you did choose. As new opportunities become available in the future, please keep me in mind."

To Get Constructive Feedback for Future Interviews

What to say if you didn't get the job and would like some feedback from the hiring manager:

> "Ms. Employer, thank you once again for interviewing me for your recent opening. It's the kind of position I hope to land one day. If you're willing, I'd appreciate any feedback you could give me on how to better present myself, or how to strengthen my background so that in the future I will be more qualified for this kind of job. Please phone or e-mail me with any ideas, and I thank you in advance for your input."

What to say when you're provided feedback:

> "Thank you. I'll consider that."

To Follow Up a Few Months After Interviewing for a Job You Didn't Get

What to say when you check back with a potential employer a few months after you interviewed for a job you didn't get:

> "Hello, Ms. Employer. It's [YOUR NAME], just calling to say hello and to check in with you about any upcoming opportunities in your organization. When I interviewed with you a few months ago, I was especially excited about the possibility of working with you and helping [ORGANIZATION NAME] achieve its goals. Please keep me in mind. I can be reached at [PHONE NUMBER]."

To Address Your Pregnancy During an Interview

What to say in an interview if you're visibly pregnant:

> "Ms. Hiring Manager, I'd like to take a minute to talk with you about my maternity leave and child-care plans as they would relate to how I would handle this job. Is this a good time?"

To Buy More Time in Making a Decision About a Job Offer

What to say if you need more time to make a decision on a job offer:

> "Mr. Hiring Manager, I have a personal matter that I need to resolve in the next two weeks. Would it be possible for me to postpone giving you my decision until [DATE]?"

What to say if you're pressed to provide details about your "personal matter":

> "I feel that this matter is one that is better kept to myself. I hope you can respect my privacy on this issue."

To Negotiate Pay to Match or Beat Another Offer

What to say if you are trying to increase pay for a job you want, when you've been offered another job that pays more:

> "Ms. Hiring Manager, I've been offered another job with pay that is slightly more in line with my worth in the market. My first choice would be to work for you. I wanted to check with you on the chance that your company could match or improve on my other offer."

Index

practicing for interviews,
57–64, 115–123
pregnancy, addressing in
interviews, 172–173, 193–194,
200
preparation. *See also*
researching
for behavioral interviews,
85–94
building confidence,
95–103
contacting hiring
managers, 9–16
for following up, 20
identifying key skill areas,
25–35
practicing for interviews,
57–64, 115–123
researching company/
industry, 49–56
for "tell me about yourself"
questions, 65–74
for traditional interviews,
75–84
visualizing ideal job, 3–8
What, How, and Proof
stories, 37–48
presentation format interviews,
116
promotion. *See* self-promotion

Q

questions
behavioral interview
questions, list of, 90–91
for interviewers, 129–130,
197

negative questions,
responding to, 81
positive questions,
responding to, 81
postponing, 194–195
"tell me about yourself"
questions, 65–74
tips for handling, 117–120,
195–196
traditional interview
questions, list of, 78–79
"why should we hire you?"
questions, 127–128,
196–197

R

rejection
causes for, 161–162
fear of, 141
following up after, 199
responding to, 159–167,
199
religious beliefs, discussing in
interviews, 80–81, 119, 194
remembering names of
interviewers, 117
researching. *See also*
preparation
company/industry, 49–56,
193
follow-up contact person,
19–20
ideal jobs, 5–7
potential employers, 6
responsibilities. *See* skills
resumes, writing effective, 6

Have No Fear: More

CaReeR CowaRd's Guides

Are Coming!

You've read this book and you're brimming with confidence about your upcoming job interviews. But now you might need a helping hand with other career and job search issues. No problem! Just look for these upcoming additions to the *Career Coward's* series!

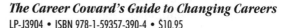

The Career Coward's Guide to Changing Careers
LP-J3904 • ISBN 978-1-59357-390-4 • $10.95

- Identify several great-fit career options.
- Make a confident choice about the best career.
- Create a fun, doable career-change plan.
- Transition into your new career smoothly and successfully.

The Career Coward's Guide to Resumes
LP-J3911 • ISBN 978-1-59357-391-1 • $10.95

- Determine what to include on your resume for great results.
- Develop your unique experiences into powerful resume content.
  - Follow a foolproof process for creating a high-results resume.
- Write outstanding cover letters in just minutes.

The Career Coward's Guide to Job Searching
LP-J3928 • ISBN 978-1-59357-392-8 • $10.95

- Find up to 70 percent more excellent job opportunities.
- Discover easy (and fearless) methods for networking.
- Take the guesswork out of how to job search successfully.
- Learn how to connect with employers that are just right for you.

The Career Coward's Guide to Career Advancement
LP-J3935 • ISBN 978-1-59357-393-5 • $10.95

- Define motivating, rewarding career paths and goals.
- Master the art of negotiating with bosses and decision makers.
- Develop ordinary jobs into extraordinary career opportunities.
- Implement small career improvements that yield huge results.

America's Career Publisher

See www.jist.com for details and release dates.